Lynn MacKenzie

The Tear Catcher

God's Hand in Your Heartache

WINEPRESS **WP** PUBLISHING

To my children,

Blake and Nicole

You've reminded me what it means to have a childlike
faith during hard days, and you've demonstrated a total
dependence on God to carry you through the storms in life.

I have learned so much from both of you.

Know that always
. . . I will love you
"Bunches of bunches and loads of loads."

To my husband whom I will always love,

Bruce

Through your life and now your death, you have
taught me how to laugh, love, and live again.
I no longer wait for the storms in my life to pass; rather,
I've learned to dance in the rain.

Thank you for being my dance partner—this side of heaven.

WinePress Publishing (PO Box 428, Enumclaw, WA 98022) functions only as book publisher. As such, the ultimate design, content, editorial accuracy, and views expressed or implied in this work are those of the author.

Unless otherwise noted, all Scriptures are taken from the *Holy Bible, New International Version®, NIV®*. Copyright © 1973, 1978, 1984 by the International Bible Society. Used by permission of Zondervan. All rights reserved.

Scripture quotations marked NLT are taken from the *Holy Bible, New Living Translation,* copyright © 1996. Used by permission of Tyndale House Publishers, Inc., Wheaton, Illinois 60189. All rights reserved.

ISBN 13: 978-1-57921-941-3
ISBN 10: 1-57921-941-1
Library of Congress Catalog Card Number: 2007941233

Contents

Foreword

Everyone has a story to tell. There isn't a person on this earth without a story of his or her own. What makes mine unique? It is the invaluable wealth of knowledge and insight into God's heart and mind that my family received during our cancer journey.

This book is about the life changing events that happened to us when no escape could be found. We were unable to run, hide, or outsmart our circumstances. Just when life for the MacKenzie's seemed to be as good as it could get, my husband, Bruce, was diagnosed with terminal cancer. He was 39. Immediately the cry of his heart became, "Make it all about you God, all about you."

My cry was different.

I prayed that God would give me the eyes to see His presence in every situation—the visible, as well as the invisible. I needed to see God in the midst of our fears. To feel comfort in knowing He was there and I wasn't alone. The lessons learned were immeasurable. I said a simple prayer and God answered it, many times in unconventional ways. Often when people suffer and don't see God in the equation, they "go it alone." We needed God. We let Him know that, and He never let us down.

Our journey showed us the multifaceted character of God. Through our suffering, we learned to submit, which ultimately led to surrender. I discovered how God can take the nothingness in our lives and turn it into something beautiful. He not only cares about the smallest of details, but also has a sense of humor and loves to surprise us. God, full of grace and mercy, desperately wants to hold us and catch our tears. With His help, I was able to see beyond our suffering and experience His immense and unconditional love.

I could have chosen to become angry and bitter; instead, I chose to let God take my broken and shattered pieces, hold them, and gently put them back together. In His wisdom, strength, gentleness, and love, He began to mold me.

During Bruce's cancer journey, I sent out e-mail updates to family and friends. By sharing our story, strangers told us how they were encouraged and touched. A pattern evolved. The stories had a common thread; simply, it was suffering. My life will never be the same. I have found a peace that surpasses my understanding, and I've discovered joy in a new journey. I could not have reached this destination on my own; it has only been through the grace of God and love of Jesus Christ that I arrived at this place. Each day I choose to move forward.

Today is the only day we know we have for sure. Don't wait until death to live. Live each day as if it's your last, and the end of each day to reflect you've lived your best.

It changed me; it can change you too.

Acknowledgments

First and foremost, I am thankful to God for being the rock that provided protection when the storms my family and I experienced seemed unbearable. His warm embrace held me, keeping me stable and secure when life wanted to knock me down and crush me. His gentle hand caught every tear we cried and dried each eye, over and over again. He was my blanket of comfort, my voice of reason, my spiritual guide, and greatest source of wisdom. He provided me with a peace that surpasses my human understanding and saw me through a very turbulent time in my life, and for that I am grateful.

To my children, Blake and Nicole, who have been one of my greatest anchors of strength. Their support for the completion of this book has been unwavering, and their encouragement kept me going even when I had doubts.

Our families have been amazing. Mom, what can I say—I love you more than words can say on this page. You've always been there for me, and you and Dad taught me how to love unconditionally as Christ loves us. Bruce's parents, Mal and Donna (Donna recently joined Bruce in heaven), have been the best father and mother-in-law a girl could ever hope for. You've welcomed me into your family as a daughter, and I thank God for blessing me with you in my life and for how you wholeheartedly gave your blessing the day I married your son. To my brothers, Dean and Dale, thank you for always being there for your little sister and for loving Bruce as a brother. To Bruce's brother, Chuck, who stood by Bruce and provided strength at a very scary time in our lives. And finally Kyle, who attended every doctor appointment possible, treatment, surgery, or anything else that pertained to her brother Bruce. Thank you from the bottom of my heart for your support, for the home-away-from home that you and John provided, for your prayers, and for being the "800-pound guerilla" when needed to get tough with the medical community or whoever else needed someone of great strength. You have a special place in my heart and will always be my "seester."

I thank all our other family members who demonstrated the true meaning of "family" and coming together in love and support. Pastor Paul, you have been such a blessing to our family. Thank you for always being there, and for providing spiritual wisdom and support to our family. But even beyond that, thank you for being a friend and confidant to Bruce over the years. To Paul Froland, who was Bruce's partner in the *Men of Faith* ministry, an incredible friend, and who shared the same passion Bruce had in surrendering all for the cause of Christ.

To all who helped in the editing and reading through of this book: my son, Blake; Mom; and Carmen Britz, who spent countless hours at our house editing and dreaming of the greater ministry of *I Win Ministries*. To Marj Maurer, Joanne Keck, Bobbi Schroeder, Jennifer and Terry Kurash, Gay Zyvoloski, Bob Kendall, and Lavonne Heise—I learned from all of you and took every comment to heart. To my coach and mentor, Judy (Baer) Duenow, who kept after me to always raise the bar and never settle for anything less as a writer.

To all who sent cards and letters, telephoned, came for visits, brought meals, offered up a multitude of prayers, and helped carry our burden in some small way—you have blessed our lives forever. To Cameron Schroeder, Dale Kuklok, Bill Eichhoff, and Paul Froland, the team of guys that came to our home every Wednesday for eleven months to pray with Bruce, I thank you. Your sacrifice of time meant more to Bruce and me than words can say. To our church family, the women who prayed for us in my Bible Study Fellowship groups, and the *Women in the Middle Christ Care* Bible study group who helped me sort out and listen to the voice of truth during my healing process and while writing this book. To the music teams at church; Bruce's alumni house co-workers at St. Cloud State University; Trinity Lutheran Church and Good Shepherd Community, who sponsored the benefit for Bruce—you've all made such an amazing impact on my family's life.

To my dear college friends, fondly known as the "Four Seasons"—Marj and Mike Maurer and their sons, Brooks and Luke; Tammy and Doug Mielke and their daughters, Janet and Jena—you have become family to us over the past twenty-something years and have been right beside us through thick and thin. We love you all so much. To our neighbors, the Scofields, who've shown us what real neighborly love is over the years, just as God intended. To all involved with Trinity Lutheran School, which now is Prince of Peace Lutheran School—to God be the glory for all the seeds that have been or ever will be planted through the Christian education that is taught there. May His name alone be glorified.

Lastly, I thank God daily for blessing my life with Bruce. For his focus on others, his love for me and the kids, and his even greater love for the Lord. Bruce was always about getting on with God's work and would ask us all what we were waiting for if God called us today to do something for Him. Bruce encouraged me to write someday; that kept me moving forward in writing this book. In honor and memory of Bruce—this one's for you, honey.

Chapter 1

The Puzzle Piece

L ong, steep, concrete stairs led the way as I walked behind
the casket in a haze. It seemed impossible that the funeral
was over. I was about to bury my 40-year-old husband. *Was this
really happening?*

It was a beautiful spring day. Music from the church flooded
the streets. The warmth of the sun penetrated the very core of
my being. Pausing for a moment, I inhaled deeply, trying to
fill every crevice in my lungs with the invigorating air. When
we arrived at my vehicle, my brother Dale commandeered the
driver's seat, and I slipped into the passenger's side. My two
children and Dale's wife sat in the back of the car. We waited as
the church emptied.

To my left I watched a steady stream of people pour out of
the church. Many gathered on the sidewalks to comfort each
other. Others clumped together, erupting into laughter as they
shared stories. The rest hurried to their cars to get in line for
the drive to the cemetery. I don't recall the conversations that
carried on, but I observed in amazement as people interacted
with one another.

How could this be? I thought. *Only one year ago everything in
our life was great.*

Glancing to my right, I saw an unfamiliar man walking toward my car. Our friend Jim followed. Instinctively, I put the car window down.

"Hello Lynn. You don't know me, but my name is Craig Moore. I am Jim's pastor. I'm sorry to hear about Bruce's death. People at our church have been praying for Bruce and your family ever since we heard about Bruce's cancer. When Jim told me that Bruce went home to heaven, I felt a strong sense that God wanted me to give you or tell you something. I didn't get much sleep last night, because I was in prayer, asking God what He wanted me to do or say."

In a closed fist he held his hand over mine.

"After a lot of prayer, I felt God wanted me to give you this."

His grip relaxed, and something tiny fell into my opened palm. Examining the item a little more closely, I realized it was a small puzzle piece. The bright yellow colors reminded me of a field of sunflowers on a sunny day. As I held the tiny puzzle piece, Pastor Craig continued, "I'm supposed to tell you this is all you see right now. One by one, God will give you more pieces to the puzzle, which will eventually start to form a picture. However, I must also caution you. You may never see the completed picture until you die and go to heaven. This probably doesn't make much sense right now, but eventually it will."

At a loss for anything intelligent to say, I looked up at Pastor Craig and said, "Thank you." He nodded and silently slipped away.

Staring at the small, yellow puzzle piece cradled in my palm, I wondered about its significance. I flipped it over and over with my fingertips. I somehow knew this odd event would one day make sense. In His own way and time, God would reveal it to me. Until then, I'd just have to wait. In deep thought, my mind began whirling as memories inundated me. *What brought me here, to a place I never thought I'd be?*

Then, I remembered . . .

• Chapter 2 •

Life Changing News

The News

Life as we knew it in mid-suburbia seemed picture perfect. Rolling along at a pretty good clip, with two kids, full careers, a house, the yard, and a cat we couldn't have squeezed one more thing into our hectic lives; that is until life suddenly came to a screeching halt.

We were spending the weekend at my mom's and getting ready for church. Bruce complained about not feeling well. In fact, the night before he had slept in the recliner downstairs, because the pain he was experiencing in his back was so intense. The weekend wasn't turning out as I expected. Sunday was my birthday, and Bruce wasn't himself. He usually was so helpful, funny, and energetic. Extreme back pains and feeling unusually tired were getting the best of him. Because he was under a lot of stress at work due to a recent promotion, I began to wonder if it was starting to affect him physically.

Bruce was the executive director of development at the university where we met. He worked from sun up to sun down. He was consumed at work, and when he wasn't at the university, he was leading the effort to build a new Lutheran school that our children would attend. I was the interim administrator at the school. It was enormously challenging, and I hoped it was only for a one-year term.

Like most birthdays in our family, I assumed mine would be no different and certain family traditions would be followed. Maybe they'd sing the birthday song to me. But no, no song, no birthday wishes, no breakfast made for me—nothing! When I asked my twelve-year-old son if he was going to get his cereal before church, he looked at me and replied, "I thought you were going to get it for me, Mom."

If ever there was a time I wanted to go on strike that was it! It wasn't until during the sermon at church that my husband reached over, touched my shoulder, and mouthed, "Happy birthday." My assumption was correct, they actually did forget!

After church and a nice dinner at mom's, we left on the 60-mile drive home. Upon arrival, we dropped the kids off and immediately left to a scheduled meeting to interview a potential permanent administrator for the school. It had been a long year; the terrorist attack of September 11th started things off, and if I ever wanted a birthday present, it was for this candidate to replace me in my interim position.

My birthday came and went. I regretted my behavior and feeling sorry for myself. As time passed, I would see how God gives us the desires of our heart whether we deserve it or not, but I'll explain that later.

The next day, Bruce visited his physician and then called me at school to tell me something was wrong. The chest x-ray revealed that his right chest cavity was all white. It was called a *pleural effusion.*

"What's that?" I asked.

"They said the wall between the lung and the chest cavity is filled with fluid."

"What kind of fluid is it? Is it bad? Is it pneumonia?"

Pneumonia was what I was hoping for. *After all, that would be a quick fix,* I thought.

I accompanied Bruce to an appointment with a pulmonary specialist for a procedure called a *thoracentesis* to find out what the strange fluid was. This was an introduction to a long series of tests to come. A long needle was inserted into Bruce's back to reach the chest wall. Attached to the needle was a long, flexible tube designed to extract fluid that was connected to a one-quart glass bottle. The procedure didn't take long. Half a quart of fluid was retrieved from Bruce's chest. The brave soldier in me took over, and I was amazed that I didn't pass out. Bruce was incredible. He hardly flinched. He actually carried on a conversation with the doctor.

Jokingly, I commented, "The fluid looks like a red ale beer, with foam to boot."

The doctor didn't laugh and got right down to business. Either it was his personality, or he was really concerned. He questioned Bruce about his family and medical history. Then the doctor ended with a frightening list of possible reasons for the pleural effusion. The severity of his condition hadn't hit me.

Returning home, I decided to do the modern thing and hop on the Internet to research pleural effusion. It was getting late, so I took the printed material up to bed to read before we turned out the lights. Everything I read was terrible. I discovered the fluid could be caused from kidney or heart failure, a tumor, blood disease . . . the list went on. If I could have chosen any one of them for my husband, I would have asked for a new list. I put my research aside and never picked it up again.

What was happening? My husband was healthy, well liked, had a good job, and was active in the community and in our church. How could something so bad happen to someone so good—to my other half? I don't believe one can fully understand the pain a spouse feels until they are in a similar situation.

Matthew 19:5 says, "For this reason a man will leave his father and mother and be united to his wife, and the two will become one flesh."

One flesh.

Somehow that took on a new meaning; I understood what this verse was saying. When Bruce hurt, I hurt. The pain gnawed at me. I ached in the depths of places I never knew existed. *What's the reason for this God? Why now? My heart hurts. Can you feel my pain? Do you even hear me? Where are you? Please answer me.*

A CAT scan was scheduled a number of days later to find out the source of the fluid. It was an incredibly blustery day, and just like the weather outside, my inside was churning. Waiting for Bruce to complete yet another procedure, I scanned my surroundings. The waiting room chairs were filled with people of all ages. Muffled sounds filled the air as people conversed. It wasn't that I couldn't understand what they were saying, but in a strange way it felt like I was living out a dream, yet looking from the outside in.

Am I really here? Or is this a dream?

Feeling surreal, I pondered why others were there; I wondered what their stories were. Tears threatened to trickle down my face, but with every ounce of strength I could muster, I fought them back. Bruce and I originally had planned to take each of our secretaries out for lunch that day, because it was Secretaries Day. With the scheduled CAT scan, we decided to delay the lunches for one day.

Unexpected interruptions on Thursday made work for both of us exceptionally busy. Lunch never happened that day either. Postponing our lunch date again seemed the logical thing to do. Relieved, Bruce went home for lunch. He felt incredibly tired. He ate and was about to take a short nap when his cell phone rang. It was Doctor Shuster, the Pulmonologist. In a very short conversation, Bruce's future drastically changed.

Slapping his cell phone shut, Bruce fell to his knees and cried out in a loud voice, "Oh God, help me. God, this has to be all about you. It has to be all about you in me, about you through me, and about you in everything I am and do. There is nothing within me to get through this. Make it about you God, all about you." After Bruce spent those agonizing moments before his Lord—which he referred to as his "Job Moment"—he told me he found himself asking a question he never thought he'd ask. "How do I tell my wife this news? Oh God, carry me. Give me the words to say to Lynn. I love her so much."

Not long after 1:00 P.M., the first grade teacher came upstairs to the main office.

"Bruce is here and wants to see you right away."

I knew the news couldn't be good; after all, he was here in person.

"Oh God, please make what I'm about to hear not be the bad news I feel is coming."

An enormous pit filled my stomach. I couldn't get to Bruce quickly enough. Tears were welling up in my eyes, and it felt like someone had their hands around my throat, causing me to choke. Bruce was standing outside my office. Wearing a suit, shiny black dress shoes, and his beautiful, long, black, wool coat, he looked so handsome. I walked ahead of him into my office and closed the door. As I turned toward Bruce, he grabbed my hands and looked into my eyes. Without hesitation he said, "Dr. Shuster called and said the cause of my back pain is stemming from tumors . . . and they are presenting themselves in multiple places."

Struggling to get the air I needed to breathe, I replied, "What does that mean—multiple places?"

Suddenly my mind recoiled back to another time. Eleven years earlier, my dad had died of colon cancer. His cancer presented itself in multiple places too. *Who did they take me for, a fool? I had traveled this road before, I knew better.* The news I was hearing was the worst possible news. *Why Lord? Why now? Why would you want to risk Bruce's life at a time when he can do so much for you?*

I didn't understand.

Please, someone, wake me up. What about the kids? How will we tell our children their dad has tumors in multiple places? I knew it had to be cancer. What an ugly thing to say.

Later that evening we told the kids. It was one of the hardest thing the two of us have ever done. I'll never forget their reactions.

Nicole cried.

Insistently Blake inquired, "Dad, are you going to die?"

The Minnows

Blake had a scheduled Boy Scout weekend at Camp Ripley on Friday. In spite of the news, we decided we would all keep as much normalcy as possible in our lives. *Nicole was another story.*

After school, Blake got into the car and held a plastic container full of water and three minnows that had been given to him from a classmate. I asked Blake, "Who will take care of these fish while you're gone for the weekend?"

He simply responded, "Nicole."

Inwardly, I was upset he had brought the minnows home. I knew what was going to happen, but I reminded myself that some lessons in life must be experienced. On our way home, we stopped at the local grocery store to pick up goldfish food. Bruce met us at home and helped Blake finish packing for his weekend trip, then they left together. On their way to meet the other scouts they stopped at McDonald's so Blake could grab a bite to eat before he left. It was also an opportunity for Bruce to have some time alone with his son. I stayed home with Nicole. At the innocent age of nine, she was excited about her new responsibility. First, she needed to put her pets in fresh water and a bigger container.

"Will an ice cream pail work, Mom?"

"Sure."

Out came an ice cream pail. Before we even put the minnows in their new home, I could tell one of them was in trouble and possibly a second. Nicole, on the other hand, was simply too excited to notice anything unusual. Once the fish were in their new home, Nicole finally noticed that one minnow was floating on its side and not moving. A second one struggled. After much persuasion, Nicole let me scoop the dead one out. It didn't take long before the second one lay motionless.

By now, Nicole was getting concerned and thought she could help. She opened the utensil drawer in the kitchen and retrieved a butter knife. Gently, she tapped the fish that lay on its side with the butter knife. Immediately the fish "came around" and started to swim again. Within the hour, it was clear the second fish was dead, and the third one now struggled. Nicole became hysterical. Screaming at the last minnow, she cried, "Fight little fish, you've gotta fight . . . you can't die! Don't die! Fight! Promise me you'll fight! You can't die . . . not now! Not ever! Fight . . . Fight! Don't die!"

As the last minnow stopped struggling and lay motionless, Nicole's sobs escalated. I had to physically pick her up and carry her into the living room. We sat on the couch. As I held her on my lap and cradled her in my arms, she buried her head in my chest and sniveled, "Fight, don't die . . ." Her little body shook as my own tears fell upon her head. Holding her tightly and rocking back and forth, I tried to reassure her everything would be okay.

Suddenly her whimpering turned into, "Daddy, don't give up, Daddy, you've got to fight . . . Daddy don't die." Her words pierced my heart. I cried harder, held on tighter, and together we rocked until Bruce came home. All the comfort in the world I gave her that afternoon couldn't take away the fear and anguish Nicole was feeling.

When Bruce arrived, I told him what had transpired. I thought it strange how three simple minnows unleashed Nicole's unconscious fear. We were exhausted from crying, and I had no desire to cook. Upbeat, Bruce said, "Nicole, why don't you pick out a restaurant, and we'll eat out tonight."

Barely finishing his sentence, Nicole seemed to get a second wind, and with swollen eyes, she looked at her Daddy and blurted out, "Daddy, I'm hungry for a steak, and I want to go to Timber Lodge Steakhouse."

Being the softy Bruce was with his little girl, he said, "Then Timber Lodge it is!"

The "News" Continues

While waiting at Timber Lodge for Bruce's sister, Kyle, and her husband, John, to join us, Bruce's cell phone rang. "Good evening, Timber Lodge Steak House," Bruce quipped, thinking it was Kyle.

A man cleared his throat and said, "Ah, hello . . . this is Dr. Shuster, calling for Bruce MacKenzie."

Needless to say, Bruce was eating crow! Knowing it was the call we were waiting for, Bruce walked outside the restaurant for privacy. Dr. Shuster shared the results of Bruce's additional tests, which confirmed our greatest fears. Bruce learned his tumors had spread to his liver and bones. Due to the urgency of these findings, Dr. Shuster scheduled a liver biopsy for the following Monday and a bone scan for Wednesday.

Putting on a grand front, Bruce returned to the booth. He confirmed what we already knew: there were several tumors around his lung area, and they were presenting themselves in multiple places. He casually added that he was scheduled to have a liver biopsy and a bone scan the next week. He never admitted to the spread of the tumors.

Once again, I knew better. *A liver biopsy? Come on! No one has a liver biopsy unless there is something in there to biopsy!* Unfortunately, my questions would go unanswered because it was the weekend.

On Sunday, we were invited to our neighbors' for dinner. The laid back afternoon soon led into evening. Cherie and I played cribbage, while Alan and Bruce watched a baseball game on TV. Though it was relaxing, there seemed to be an elephant in the room that no one wanted to address. It was apparent Bruce and I didn't want to go home because we'd have to face reality, and frankly, life really sucked about then. Ever since the phone call at Timber Lodge, Bruce knew the tumors were in his liver and bones, but he deliberately hid this little known fact from the rest of us so we could have one final weekend where we didn't have to deal with reality.

The next day, Bruce checked into the St. Cloud Hospital for the liver biopsy. I can still smell the sterile scent of the hospital and see the various shades of the cold, grey metal. I didn't want to be there.

The biopsy confirmed that, indeed, Bruce had cancer. It was time to meet with an Oncologist. What we knew up to that point was the cancer had already spread from the lungs to the bones and liver. Half of his right lung had collapsed from the pressure of the fluid around his lung. We were hoping the Oncologist would offer a glimmer of hope and some direction. After all, he was the expert.

Introducing himself and shaking our hands, he sat down and dove right in. He was abrasive and without any test results or scans in front of him, he confidently pronounced our fate.

"Bruce, you have cancer. It's already at Stage IV and is a glandular cancer called *Adenocarcinoma*. It is highly suspected that it's of lung primary, meaning that it may have originated in your lungs. If you respond to chemotherapy, it may lengthen the time you have left. But if you don't respond to the chemotherapy or do nothing, you would be lucky to have approximately a two month prognosis."

Wow! How could the doctor tell you that news on your first office visit? He didn't even have all the reports and scans in front of him to confirm the prognosis.

Looking down at the floor, he said, "I'm sorry."

Bruce and I were stunned, yet we looked at each other and smiled anyway. Little did our doctor know we were not buying his pronouncement that day, because we knew that God was much bigger than any problems we faced.

Chapter 3

Seeing His Presence

The Presence

The first days after the news dragged on like a never-ending nightmare. Bruce struggled to fight his own battles in dealing with the myriad effects of cancer. I faced a different type of battle. Needing to be strong for the kids and Bruce was a challenge. Blake and Nicole were afraid to go to their Daddy and burden him with daily issues. It was almost as if they thought by doing so they'd ultimately make him worse. Shouldering the heavy responsibility of keeping everything together seemed nearly impossible.

Feeling ill equipped and overwhelmed with carrying this load, I poured my heart out to God. I knew in my head that God would always be with me, but fear began to cloud my mind and eyes with confusion and lies. I began to doubt and question. Feeling a sense of panic, I prayed that God would not only give me the eyes to see His presence in every visual sense, but also in the invisible. Nothing I could see before me made sense. Exercising a blind faith seemed to be my only option.

Give me the eyes to see your presence, Lord.

That was my prayer. That was my cry.

The presence of the Lord never ceased to amaze me. I can see His guidance even in my office on the day when Bruce grabbed my hands, looked me in the eyes, and told me that he had tumors that were "presenting themselves in multiple places." Bruce should have been at a restaurant with his secretaries honoring Secretaries Day when he received that shocking phone call. Thank God he was in our quiet home when that call came. When he drove to school to tell me about the phone call, it was clear to see God's presence encompassing us. I shouldn't have been there either, because I was supposed to take my secretary out to lunch. It became obvious that God was orchestrating everything.

After Bruce told me the news, I needed to take care of a few items at school so I could go home with him. I hated leaving Bruce alone in my office, so I suggested he call his good friend, Paul Froland, and tell him the news.

What was about to happen was simply amazing. Bruce dialed Paul's number on his cell phone, and Paul answered. In Bruce's left ear he could hear the laughter of small children outside the door to my office. In Bruce's right ear he could hear Paul's voice talking to him, but strangely it sounded like the same children's voices and laughter coming from the background of his conversation with Paul. It was almost as if Bruce was hearing these precious young voices in stereo.

Perplexed, Bruce asked, "Paul, where are you?"

"I'm at school for Hannah's preschool field trip."

"Where are you in the school, Paul?"

"I'm right outside Lynn's office."

Wow, Bruce really did hear the same children's voices in stereo! Surprised, he eagerly responded, "Well, imagine that, I'm right inside Lynn's office, and I've heard from the doctor. Could you please come in here?" Within moments, Paul stood before Bruce. After sharing the news, he embraced Bruce and they prayed together. Having Paul physically there was exactly what Bruce needed. Once again, God in his amazing grace was taking care of all the finite details.

In the meantime, I went upstairs to inform my secretary I needed to leave and why. I was in tears and some of the teachers that didn't have children in their classrooms gathered around me. My head was spinning as I told them what had transpired. Suddenly, my dear friend Laurie Gerchy walked into the school office. Immediately, I pulled her into the nearby empty first grade classroom and poured out my heart. Before I could even think of my children, Laurie did.

"What about your kids, Lynn?"

Alarmed, I replied, "Kids? Oh no, what am I going to do about the kids? They don't know yet. How are we going to tell them?" Emotions flooded over me, and my heart felt like it was going to rip out of my chest.

"Don't worry about your kids. I'll take Blake and Nicole home with me. I'll feed them and then bring them home around 7:30 tonight. You and Bruce need some time alone to call family and to digest what just happened. The kids will be fine with our family; you can tell them later."

Ahh, momentary relief.

Laurie seemed to fall right out of the sky and appear at the very instant I needed her. Not only was she there to provide a shoulder to cry on, but also she was there to take our children. What were the chances of Paul and Laurie being at the school, in the exact places when we needed them most? This was no coincidence. If we couldn't see God's hand in this nightmare by now, then we were blind.

Before we went home we wanted to tell our pastor. Pastor Paul Cloeter was more than a pastor to Bruce; he was a good friend. From my office, we phoned the church, which was just across the alley from the school. The office administrator told us Pastor Paul wasn't in and wouldn't be in for the rest of the day. We left a message for him to call us right away. Bruce left the school in his car, and I was gearing up to follow. No sooner had I put the key in the ignition than Pastor Paul drove up to the church. Relieved, I immediately called Bruce.

"Turn around, wherever you are, Pastor Paul just drove up." I put my car window down and yelled, "Pastor Paul, wait up! Bruce will be here in a minute, and we need to talk to you. We have the results of the medical tests we've been waiting for." Within minutes Bruce arrived. We all walked into Pastor Paul's office and sat down. He could tell whatever we heard couldn't be good news. Bruce led the conversation, and again I felt like I was suffocating. The air was thick and stagnant.

Was I actually choking or just fighting back another round of tears? Oh Lord, wake me up!

I don't remember everything Bruce told Pastor Paul, but there is one thing that will forever resonate in my memory. The three of us sat on chairs in a triangle facing each other. Pastor Paul leaned forward, his forearms resting on his knees. Concern and sadness enveloped his face. It was almost as if he was searching for words to comfort us, but he couldn't find them.

Interrupting the silence, Bruce confidently stated, "I look at it this way—I win either way. I win if God heals me physically and I'm able to stay here on earth for a while longer with my family and friends. And, I win if God calls me home to spend eternity with Him. But hey, either way, I *win!*"

Stunned, Pastor Paul and I were speechless. We just looked at Bruce in amazement. He astounded me with his prophetic wisdom. It was so deep and passionate, and Bruce's heart exposure to God had a way of refocusing us. From the very moment Bruce said he won either way, I realized that I had no reason to question. I didn't even have any right to complain. God didn't cause this mountain to be placed smack dab in the middle of our lives, but he did allow it. It was now up to us to trust God and let Him lead us on this journey.

After an emotional time spent with Pastor Paul, Bruce and I left for home. Reality loomed on the horizon, and we needed to tell our children. My car seemed to be moving in slow motion as I drove home along Benton Drive. My thoughts wandered aimlessly. Startled, I realized my cell phone was ringing. It was Bruce. He was concerned about me, and by the sound of my voice, he could tell I was crying. He offered to turn around and pick me up if I'd just pull over. Managing to gain my composure, I responded, "It's okay honey, I can see through my tears."

The First Date

Even though God's presence was evident from the very beginning of Bruce's diagnosis, thoughts of mortality kept knocking at my mind's door, and I couldn't help but look back on our life together. Memories of our life poured in. *How did we get here? What brought us to this place?*

Bruce and I had an unusual beginning. It wasn't until my fifth and final year at St. Cloud State University that we met. I was sitting in a Speech Communications class during fall quarter, when the professor called on me to give an update about the Speech Communication Club. I was the president that year. Bruce didn't know me yet, but when the professor addressed me by name and engaged me in conversation, Bruce was impressed.

Gradually, I began to notice Bruce in class. He had already pegged me as cute but unapproachable, because, in his justified world, I was president of the "Speech Com. Club" and thus not in his ballpark—or so he thought. As the quarter progressed, so did our relationship. We began to flirt with each other. Inwardly, I wanted him to ask me out, but he seemed hesitant. In the meantime, we saved seats for each other and passed notes back and forth. We were behaving like elementary school kids with crushes, instead of mature college students waiting to conquer the world.

In January, Bruce finally got enough courage to ask me out. Well, sort of. A concert was scheduled that night on campus. I was a resident advisor for one of the dorms on campus and getting an evening off didn't come easily. I had arranged to go to the concert with another RA, but as luck would have it, at the last minute she was called to go on duty, which left me with no one to go with to the concert. Telling Bruce of my dilemma, he cowardly replied, "I suppose I could go to the concert and sit next to you."

"That would be great . . . I think."

Sit next to me? What was that? Was that his way of asking me out?

Most girls wouldn't find that approach attractive or appealing. Nonetheless, I was excited to go to the concert with Bruce. Once we arrived at the Performing Arts Center, he informed me that he had forgotten his wallet. I ended up paying for both tickets.

The concert was wonderful. But when I returned to my dorm, our date ended abruptly, as I needed to deal with a situation that affected one of the girls on my floor. Looking back on the evening, I was left to wonder if there would be a second date. Let me see: a flimsy way to ask a girl out. That's strike one. Forgetting his wallet; that's strike two. It's a good thing there wasn't a third strike, or he'd be out! He had one more chance.

The First Dance

The first date came and went, and nothing really changed. We continued playing our elementary school games, yet I longed for something more. One Sunday, as we both studied in my dorm room, Bruce asked a strange question out of the blue.

"Do you like to dance?"

"I love to dance," I replied.

Then Bruce asked me if I'd like to join him in the Muscular Dystrophy Tri-College Dance-a-Thon that was being hosted by St. Cloud State University, St. John's University, and St. Ben's University.

"I'd love to go with you," I responded.

We raised our pledges and set off for the eighteen hour dance-a-thon. It was an incredible time. Other than a few short breaks, we danced the entire eighteen hours and had a ball. While other dancers grew tired and dragged their feet, we were kicking up our heels. We danced strong until the end. When the dance finished, we sat down for a few announcements. With our backs leaning against the gym wall, Bruce turned, leaned over, and kissed me for the first time. Time stood still. I lost myself in that moment, and I forgot where I was. Dazed, I remember hearing people yelling.

"They're calling your names. Go up. You need to get up. They're calling your names!" We were so caught up in the moment that neither of us realized we had just won "Best Couple Dancers" trophies. A spotlight suddenly exposed the embrace from our first kiss. Feeling awkward, we stood up. Hand in hand, we approached the platform where the judges stood. Tired and sweaty, we smiled as the other dancers cheered and applauded. Something stirred inside us that early morning leaving St. John's University.

As Bruce drove me back to my dorm, I looked at him and said, "I think we need to talk."

"I know. Things are no longer the same, are they?"

That was a turning point in our relationship. The judges and others watched us dance all night long. Even though we never saw it, they did. For us, it just happened. We danced right into each other's hearts and simply fell in love.

• Chapter 4 •

Life's Journey on New Terrain

The E-mails Begin

From the beginning of the cancer diagnosis, our experience was overwhelming. How could we get through this journey alone? We couldn't. We needed to update family and so many others. It was beginning to feel like the telephone was surgically attached to our ears. Frankly, it was wearing on us. I saw it in my children's faces. Exhausted and knowing we needed prayer, it was time we asked for help.

E-mails—that would work. I could type a message out to the masses, say it once, everyone would hear the same thing, and the prayers from family and friends would begin immediately. Praise God for Internet technology.

Creating a group listing entitled, "Bruce's Prayer Warriors," I began to type.

Dear friends:

Greetings. I am e-mailing you to share some awful news about Bruce. We are requesting prayers. Feel free to share this e-mail with anyone willing to pray for us.

For the past several months, Bruce has been having back and breathing problems. He has doctored with chiropractors, physical therapists, and even received professional massages. Nothing was helping, and the pain he experienced was gradually getting worse. He went back to the doctor, and they finally took a chest x-ray. It revealed that his entire right lung was covered with what appeared to be a white cloud. After seeing a Pulmonologist, he was told he has a *Pleural Effusion,* which in layman's terms means water on the lungs. The culprit is a large tumor that presents itself in his back, liver, and lung area. This explains his pain. Bruce will have a liver biopsy in a few days. Our faith is strong, but in the midst of these frightening times, we need to trust that God is right beside us, even when we can't see Him. It's amazing to me, how one simple phone call can change your life. Thursday was one of the worst days of my life.

A few days later another e-mail read:

. . . Bruce found out today that the tumor is cancer. It is in his bones, lungs, and liver. That's what we know so far. The doctor wasn't sure where the cancer originated. We have an appointment with an oncologist late tomorrow. We hope to get more answers and make a treatment plan. He will need radiation and chemotherapy.

> The cancer is advanced, but we refuse to let this
> diagnosis corner us into utter despair. We know
> with God all things are possible and that is why
> we are asking you to join us in boldly praying
> for God's healing and protection.

These e-mails were the first of many. They provided a valuable venue to disseminate information to many. It also provided an avenue to share how the Lord's presence was strong despite the storms. The e-mails told of God's story by using our story.

The Radiation

After the first week of hearing the news, reality set in. We needed to make decisions. An MRI revealed that the cancer had wrapped itself around one of the vertebrae in Bruce's spinal cord. The doctor explained that if it penetrated the protective sheathing any further it would cause paralysis.

Excuse me? Now we faced a triple whammy: dealing with Bruce's spreading cancer, facing the effects of radiation and chemo, and now potential paralysis. How much more can we take? Dr. Wong, our Radiation Oncologist, ordered a second MRI, this time of the brain. We immediately traveled across town for the appointment, and the technicians were waiting for us. I thought, *These people really move fast!* However, they knew the severity of the matter that I was just beginning to understand.

The appointment was set for 4:00 P.M., and we were told to wait for the MRI films so we could bring them back to the cancer center. It was 5:30 when we returned to the center and met our Radiation Oncologist. He immediately took the films into a conference room with both of us hot on his heels. Just as he expected, the cancer had invaded Bruce's brain too. Three pea-size tumors were evident on the films.

No! I screamed in my head. *I can't take any more!*

I wanted to leave, but I couldn't. Because of the threat to the spinal cord, Bruce underwent the first radiation treatment to his spine that very afternoon.

It was now 6:00 P.M. Friday night. All the patients and most of the staff went home for the weekend. I watched the last few workers leave, thinking how lucky they were to be going home to their "normal" lives. That made me mad. Bruce and I would return to a life that was anything but normal. In fact, it was foreign. Bruce went into the procedure room for his first radiation session. I waited.

Lord, this is not fair. Why Bruce? He is your child. Always ready to listen, obey, and serve. Why down this path? Why at this time? Did we do something wrong? Are we being punished? Is this a test? Why does this cancer have to be at the end stages and in so many places? What does all this mean?

I wanted answers.

I started to cry.

Carol, Dr. Wong's nurse, walked over and leaned down beside my chair. She held my hand and didn't speak. Tears filled her eyes.

Dr. Wong came out to the waiting room. "Everything went well, and Bruce should be out soon." He paused. "Things don't look good. You should get your papers in order. Take a lot of pictures this weekend and, if you have a video recorder, take some movies too."

What did he mean when he said "get your papers in order"? Why can't people just tell you straight out what they mean?

It was good advice, but very difficult to hear.

I muttered amidst the sobs, "I don't know what our children will do without their dad. My part-time administrator position will be ending in a few months. I can't go back to work; Bruce and my children need me now more than ever. What are we going to do?"

Deafening silence flooded the room. I tried to compose myself. Dr. Wong and Carol stood motionless, except for the tears that rested in their eyes. Closing my eyes I silently prayed, "Lord, give me enough light for my next step."

The Prayer Warriors

Again, it was time to update *Bruce's Prayer Warriors*. By now the word had spread like wild fire. People all over the United States heard of his affliction. We received cards daily, the phone rang non-stop, and e-mails constantly filled our computer screen. It was encouraging to hear from people who were praying for Bruce and our family—those we knew and those we didn't know. *Bruce's Prayer Warriors* seemed to be the perfect name. It was apparent that those who knew and loved us were ready to join in the fight. Our faith was grounded and our roots deep, but the storm outside, as well as inside, continued to rage. Our children struggled with all the unanswered questions, the unfairness of it all, and overwhelming sadness. They were afraid and didn't understand why this was happening to our family.

Bruce was uninhibited and used every opportunity to witness to others. Whoever had ears to hear, Bruce shared with them. Despite the strength I saw in Bruce, however, I knew he had quiet moments of weakness and despair. We were so thankful for all God's provisions, but especially for the Prayer Warriors. Often we heard, "I wish there was something I could do, but all I can do is pray." Then pray! It's a privilege to pray and one of the most important things you can do. God delights to hear from us, and there is power in prayer.

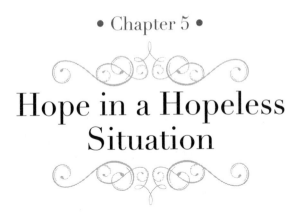

Chapter 5

Hope in a Hopeless Situation

The Hope

The first two weeks flew by in a blur. With doctor appointments, tests, adjusting to a full regimen of different medications, and starting radiation and chemotherapy, our entire world took on a new focus. Our lives were no longer our own. Clouds congregated above our heads, and the sun seemed nowhere to be found.

Finding hope in this hopeless situation seemed impossible. I'll admit it was tempting to barter and bargain with God, but we knew that God saw the big picture and we didn't. We were only a small pixel in God's global view of our lives. He knew exactly what would happen to us every minute of each day that we were blessed with. Our lives were in God's mighty, strong hands, and frankly, I couldn't think of a better place to be.

Amazingly, Bruce and I never became angry with God. Oh, we were angry. We were angry Bruce got cancer. We were scared, confused, and felt completely helpless, but we were never without hope. Despite the fear of the unknown, we knew God would walk before us. The roads we traveled were unpaved and uneven. Pebbles of all sizes came to rest in our shoes and irritated our tired feet.

In the book *See You at the Top,* Zig Ziglar wrote, "Go as far as you can see, and when you get there, you will always be able to see further." One step at a time is all any of us can take anyway. Why is there a tendency to take unnatural leaps into the darkness when faced with uncertainty? We tire more quickly and easily get off balance. I recalled when Jesus spoke to the people during His three short years of ministry and said, "I am the light of the world. Whoever follows me will never walk in darkness, but will have the light of life" (John 8:12).

Jesus wasn't talking about the physical light we see when we squint into the bright sunshine. He was talking about a much deeper kind of light. Jesus is the kind of light that sees us to the next sunrise when we cry ourselves to sleep at night. He holds us up when our body wants to crumble in surrender. He is the kind of light that doesn't lie. He exposes the darkness for what it is. He lights our path with truth when the world would rather deceive us.

We were traveling an unfamiliar road. The surrounding darkness left us helpless, but God's light within us gave us hope. Job 13:15a says, "Though he slay me, yet will I hope in him." Next to that verse in my Bible I wrote, "Even with stage four cancer!" Lost in thought I reflected back. So much had already happened; so much yet to come—many tests to face, lessons to learn, emotions to be tapped. There were so many faces of God yet to be realized, trials to be experienced, and blessing's waiting to be poured out. Then I prayed, *Lord, as we travel this road, give us a pin poke of Your light in the darkness surrounding us . . . It's all we need to see our next step.*

The Fleece Blanket

Wonderful responses and encouraging words came from so many people who supported us. You can't imagine how uplifting these were. One of the early e-mails we received eventually presented itself in a physical way.

God bless you and your family, Lynn. The Bates and Barclay families have a present that Bruce can use throughout his treatments. I don't know if you will read this today, but we would like to drop it off tonight if that is possible, so Bruce can have it in Rochester. My Mom is making it and will have it finished tonight. If you get this, please let me know if there is a good time to drop it off this evening. We won't stay. We just want you to have it.

I pray every thought I have of you, which is many! I have also given your request for prayer to my friend who is a DCE (Director of Christian Education) for *South Shore Trinity* in White Bear Lake. She is a mighty prayer warrior and has put your family on every prayer request chain she has . . . and believe me, those prayers are mighty and many.

In God's constant grace and love,
Cheri

We received this e-mail the afternoon before we traveled to the Mayo clinic in Rochester for a second opinion. That evening during supper, our good friends, Cheri and Dan Bates, brought over a beautiful hand made fleece blanket. One side was red and the other a plaid of green, blue, red, and white. Cheri's mom, Renea Barclay, had sewn it especially for Bruce, because she knew of others who had cancer and tended to get cold when they went through chemotherapy. How true that turned out to be. Bruce took that blanket wherever he went. Our cat, BoTie, also became attached to the fleece blanket. It was a part of Bruce and wherever he went, so did BoTie. The gift was ideal, because Bruce's internal thermostat went haywire. After receiving the blanket, we talked about how important it is to listen to God's small whispers. We discussed how many times we're guilty of not responding to His calling because we think we're too busy. It's easy to swat those whispers away or think we'll get around to it later. Thankfully, Renea didn't swat away the whisper to make the fleece blanket. What a joy it was for her to share her talents with someone who was hurting, and what a blessing it was for Bruce to receive the warmth the blanket provided.

No one could explain why Bruce contracted stage four cancer at just 39 years. In our humanness it just didn't make sense, but God was calling us to trust Him and travel down this road with Him. Even though we felt helpless, it was obvious that God was behind the scenes working out the smallest of details, giving us hope, even providing Bruce with warmth when he became cold. The gift of the fleece blanket showed us that even though we couldn't physically see God, we knew He was there. We couldn't run from our circumstances, but we knew we could run to God.

The Second Opinion

Things happened rapidly, and because Bruce's cancer was at such an advanced stage, we needed to make critical decisions quickly. Going to the Mayo Clinic seemed like the next logical step. Everyone agreed. We'd get the "best of the best" medical advice from the world renowned doctors at the Mayo Clinic.

They'll fix Bruce. They'll make him better. Who was I kidding? It wasn't as if they could kiss his boo-boo away. We arranged the appointment pronto. We stayed several days at a hotel next to the clinic. After hours of waiting and then finally meeting with the doctor, we learned little new information. The doctor confirmed four things: our local cancer center's chemo plan was also recommended by the Mayo Clinic; Bruce's cancer was of "lung primary," meaning it originated in the lungs; because his cancer had spread to the brain, he would not qualify for any clinical studies; and his cancer was incurable. There was comfort in getting a second opinion, nonetheless.

Adenocarcinoma is a glandular cancer. When the Mayo clinic identified its origin, we were confused because Bruce wasn't a smoker. *What was that about?* We never determined how he contracted lung cancer. There were possibilities and high probabilities, but where would these speculations, assumptions, and accusations get us? We needed to let the "whys" go and deal with reality.

We had a plan. Within a few days of our return, Bruce would receive his first regimen of chemo treatment. We were absolutely exhausted. My good friend Laurie had sent a gift bag with me and said not to open it until we arrived at the hotel. I'll never forget what it contained. There were two wine glasses, one individual, single serving size of wine for me, and a bottle of grape juice for Bruce. There was a small candle, bubble bath, a bottle of lotion, and body spray. Sticky notes were attached to each individual item carefully wrapped in tissue paper. The notes were fun to read and the gift was so thoughtful. The first night at the hotel, Bruce insisted that I take a bubble bath with the single candle and pour myself a glass of wine. He poured himself the grape juice in the wine glass and relaxed on the bed. Within minutes he was sound asleep. The small, thoughtful gifts and visits during that difficult time left a lasting impression on me. God, in His mercy, used a friend to make our bumpy road a little smoother. The giving of the gift bag during a very scary time in our lives was more than a gift to me. It was the love of a friend, all wrapped up in tissue paper.

Thank you God for friends and the little blessings they provide along the way.

The Chemotherapy

It was Mother's Day weekend, the first time in a long time that both our mothers were at our home. The last time both families were together for Mother's Day was nearly sixteen years ago at our wedding. Despite all the family and friends that came to visit, I felt so alone.

Over the weekend we took a lot of pictures and received many phone calls. Among Bruce's cell phone, my cell phone, and our landline, which had two lines, we were always talking to someone. It was exhausting to tell the story over and over again. The not-so-funny joke in our house was that the phone actually never rang, but rather it would "click" in. Often Bruce or I would say, "Just a minute, our other line just clicked in, can I put you on hold?" Sadly, we went from call to call to call from the beginning of "the news" into the days ahead. However, our children were suffering. They needed their mom and dad more than ever, and we were nowhere to be found.

The next week was filled with daily visits to the Cancer Center for radiation treatments. Bruce seemed to be tolerating the regime, but he tired easily. By now, he had officially taken a leave-of-absence from work. Physically, he was unable to sit for long periods of time, and the stairs at work were more than he could handle. The lesions on his brain were also compromising his concentration level.

In addition to receiving radiation treatments, Bruce needed to start chemo treatments as soon as possible. We took the first available date, May 10th. Thoughts immediately rushed into my head. *Not May 10th! That is our 16th wedding anniversary. He can't start chemo then! What if we don't make it to our 17th anniversary?* The future was so uncertain. Bruce didn't feel like celebrating anyway, so we decided to get started. The chemo treatment wasn't that bad. We were taken to one of the small, private rooms where the treatments were administered. Bruce sat in a recliner, and there was a TV/VCR in the room so we could watch a movie if we wanted.

Bruce slept part of the time. Chemo patients often get sleepy from the Benadryl that's administered to counter any allergic reactions they may have to the chemo drugs. As he slept peacefully, I watched him. Here was my husband on our wedding anniversary, with an IV in his arm, and near lethal drugs coursing through his veins to fight off the bad guys. I remembered walking this road before with my father and his cancer, and I feared for Bruce and the terrible reaction from chemo that he'd have to endure.

God, how I loved him.

It had been eleven years since my dad died from colon cancer. I had accompanied Mom and Dad to every doctor appointment and to as many tests and treatments as I could. We used to joke when I was pregnant with my son, Blake, that dad and I had something in common: kitchen and cooking smells bothered both of us, and we got nauseated very easily. Now I walked this journey with my husband. It felt as if my dad's journey was preparation for the road I now traveled.

As soon as the first chemo treatment ended, we were free to leave. I was prepared to take Bruce home, put him in bed, and have a pail near by. Much to our surprise, he felt quite good. It was probably because of all the steroids included in his chemo concoction. My brother Dale and his fiancée, Jayne, arrived from Eau Claire, Wisconsin, shortly after we came home. Hugs were exchanged, and then I said, "It's really great to see you two and wonderful that you came to see us, however, today is our 16th wedding anniversary, and surprisingly, Bruce is feeling quite good. We've decided to go out for dinner alone to celebrate."

"Go," Dale said. "Don't worry about us. We will take care of the kids and feed them. Enjoy!"

We went to an Italian restaurant for dinner. Bruce seemed to want to savor every moment with me. He wouldn't let go of my hands and just kept gazing into my eyes. Ever since Bruce and I first met, he would look at me and say, "Have I ever told you that you have pretty eyes?" He must have told me that at least twice a week during our marriage. Today was no exception. With our fingers entwined and Bruce's eyes locked in on mine, he repeated those ten precious words. He lovingly spoke them as if it was the first time he had said them. The words seemed to simply hang in the air along with the smell of garlic and oregano. Oh, how I loved hearing those ten precious words.

Chapter 6

This Battle Is the Lord's

The Similarities

Our family was finally starting to get our "cancer legs." My days were spent with Bruce at the doctor's office, taking him to treatments, and aiding in the survival of the curses that come with chemo and radiation. The conversations Bruce and I had during the following days were treasured. We broached a variety of topics, and he always seemed to end up relating those topics to spiritual matters. One day as I was bringing his morning pill ration, Bruce looked up at me and said, "You know, Lynn, this battle is the Lord's." Dressed in loose fitting pajamas, a sweatshirt, and sporting his tan suede slippers, Bruce proceeded with his daily routine of taking his fistfull of morning pills. Then he picked up a devotional he had next to him and continued to read. I looked at him a moment and waited—waiting for what, I wasn't sure.

"OK, Bruce . . . you're not going to make a statement like that and then just leave me hanging. What did you mean by, 'This battle is the Lord's'?"

"I was just reading about young David in the Bible when he faced the giant, Goliath. Well, I can identify with David. Like him, I'm up against the odds. He only had a few rocks in his shepherd's bag to fight the mighty giant, but that was by choice. It was only after King Saul tried to dress him in his own armor he had worn into battles that David chose to wear his own clothing." Then Bruce picked up his Bible and read 1 Samuel 17:38–40:

> "Then Saul dressed David in his own tunic. He put a coat of armor on him and a bronze helmet on his head. David fastened on his sword over the tunic and tried walking around, because he was not used to them. 'I cannot go in these, he said to Saul, because I am not used to them.' So he took them off. Then he took his staff in his hand, chose five smooth stones from the stream, put them in the pouch of his shepherd's bag and, with his sling in his hand, approached the Philistine."

Bruce explained, "Others have been trying to give me suggestions to try different things—everything from drinking a special tea, eating certain foods, taking supplements, or experimenting with other treatment methods. Just as David tried on Saul's tunic, I've been trying on others suggestions and ideas. I'm coming to the strange realization that God has uniquely prepared me for this battle. Even though I don't see it, I must fight this on my own; but ultimately, the battle is the Lord's." With that, he appeared to be done with the conversation, pulled the fleece blanket up to his chest, and snuggled in to finish his devotional. Turning around and heading back to the kitchen, I replayed our brief conversation. Ironically, there did seem to be a direct correlation between David's story and Bruce's.

In the days ahead, Bruce tried others suggestions. He found some ideas helpful, but overall, nothing really worked. Just like the armor that David tried on, Bruce found that others armament was heavy, cumbersome, and awkward. Even though they were thousands of years apart in history, their stories were similar. God prepared David to fight Goliath years before he would actually face the giant. David was a shepherd boy who learned to have a gentle, humble spirit; yet he also developed a sense of survival and leadership characteristics. Those characteristics didn't develop in him because he asked God for them; rather, God allowed them to be developed in David for a greater purpose—to prepare him for a greater plan. In his early years, he killed a bear and lion with his own hands to protect the sheep for which he was responsible. Only God could have helped him out with that one. Just as God prepared David, God prepared Bruce with other battles he faced years prior to his cancer diagnosis.

Most people weren't aware of the struggles and trials Bruce encountered earlier in his life. It was as if those battles prepared him for what he now faced. I'll explain that in just a bit. What I've learned from David is that despite the giants in our lives, God has prepared us for the battles we will endure whether we realize it or not. I've also learned not to get discouraged if other people's armament doesn't fit.

Bruce proudly wore the armament God gave him. God's unique armament was perfect. He knew the battles Bruce would face and how to prepare him. Bruce saw God's faithfulness, and while taking one day at a time, he continued to move forward in faith, knowing that ultimately the battle was the Lord's.

The Application

The e-mails and cards that arrived were spiritual food for our journey. I'll never forget one unique e-mail that we received. It read:

Hello Bruce . . .

I learned Thursday noon from Cameron Schroeder
that you have openings for Prayer Warriors!
I'd like to apply for an open spot.
I'm sure you have many applicants,
but I have experience and can start immediately.
I am fully equipped with a helmet of salvation,
breast plate of righteousness,
a belt of truth, sword of the Spirit, shield of faith,
and I wear the Gospel shoes.
I can give the prayer of agreement under fire, and
I know how to exercise my power and
authority over the enemy.
I require neither pay nor rations,
because all my needs are supplied by my
Supreme Commander.
What do you say—do we have a deal?

Be at peace, Bruce; many are praying for you.
Dick Molohon

This e-mail fascinated me, because I immediately recognized where Dick found the application portion. It was Scripture! Ephesians 6:10–18 talks about the armor of God. How beautiful it is to personalize Scripture. That's what God wants for all His children. Personalize His Word! The Bible is for everyone. Our family needed to claim the promises that God had given to us and to learn from God's instructions in Scripture. He gives us all we need. He had already provided the wisdom and direction for us to get through our trials and struggles. We just needed to pick it up, read it, and then live it.

Bruce and our family were in a battle for our lives. We all needed to put on God's armor for protection from the devil's attacks. Good soldiers don't walk into battle with street clothes and a backpack. That would be foolish. Instead they dress in gear from head to toe, armed with weapons, and trained in how to "think" like a soldier.

I thought about times when we face tragedies in our lives and we're caught like a doe in the headlights of a car. Do we jump out of the way or stand in fright and become road-kill? We need to arm ourselves with the same type of spiritual weaponry. Battles and storms invade our lives all the time. Are we prepared? So many people asked how we were able to get through the "valley walks" we were experiencing. Simply put, on our own we couldn't. It was only because of God's armor surrounding and protecting us that we stood strong.

Since that e-mail, I try to remember this Scripture every morning when my legs swing over the side of the bed, and I prepare to get up. As my bare feet touch the floor, I am reminded to put on the armor of God. After prayer and personalizing this passage, I am ready to face the battles that await me.

Don't kid yourself. It's not as easy as it sounds when faced with trials in life. Not only will the trial itself be difficult, but the devil will take advantage of your weakened state. He will try to invade your thoughts, your heart, and your very soul. He doesn't care that you're hurting, confused, and at the end of your rope. In fact, that is the time when you are most vulnerable to his flaming arrows of deceit and deception. Satan will plant false truths in your mind like, "Well, I guess you deserved this one; look at you, God must be punishing you. He doesn't really love you. If He did, He'd take this burden from you. Where is He, huh? I don't see Him, do you? Of course not, that's because He's not here! I guess you're all alone . . ." On and on the devil continues to plant, plot, and scheme. Take heart. The devil will never win the war. He will continue to attack and may snag a few battles here and there, but the war has already been won. The victory is ours.

I was thankful for the unusual e-mail Dick sent and for reminding us that Scripture is "an ever-present help" in time of need. I no longer look at job applications in the same light. My prayer is that my life's resume will always give witness to Jesus Christ, my Supreme Commander.

God bless the Prayer Warriors.

The Friend Returned

A great gift came early on from a good friend. It was unexpected, and this particular gift touched my heart. I came home one sunny afternoon in May to find a surprise gift bag on our front steps addressed to me. As I opened it, I saw a small inspirational book, a card with a beautiful note, and a crisp $50 bill in the card. Immediately, I began to cry. Tears streamed down my face, not because of the $50 bill or the inspirational book, but because the gift bag came from a long lost, dear friend.

Three years earlier, I had met Carmen in a Bible study. I was a discussion leader for Bible Study Fellowship. We were studying the book of Romans that particular year, and Carmen had been assigned to my small group. I came to realize that she was a beautiful young woman—vibrant, full of life, and with a genuine love for her Lord. Only two weeks after we met, she was diagnosed with Stage II Hodgkin's Lymphoma. Cancer.

During that time, I got to know Carmen on a deeper level. I prayed with her, called her often, visited her in the hospital, and accompanied her to a few chemo treatments. She was close to my age, and our children were similar in age also. My heart ached for her and all that she was experiencing. I even wrote a poem titled *The Tear Catcher* for her. Its significance resonates even today.

As time went by, Carmen and I grew apart, and I had not seen or spoken to her for several years. She found out about Bruce's cancer from a mutual friend while shopping at a local grocery store. The irony struck me that I had ministered to her during her greatest need. Now after several years, God worked behind the scenes to see to it that Carmen would be a comforting minister to both Bruce and me. Praise God for his faithfulness and His omniscience.

Carmen called, sent notes, and visited often. Despite the physical distance of thirty miles, the Lord kept leading her into our lives. Bruce looked forward to her visits. As I started to tape cards we received on our walls, Bruce wanted her cards and inspirational messages next to him by his favorite chair. He wanted them close so that anytime he needed a lift or words of encouragement, her cards were accessible. Carmen radiated God's love with her presence, always pointing others to God for strength, comfort, and love. What a great friend she had become. It was increasingly apparent that God's hand was involved in bringing her back into our lives. But was there a greater purpose?

The Spring Concert

Bruce was a wonderful father. He had three priorities in his life—God, wife, and children. Everything after that would somehow fall into place, he would say.

I'll never forget the great lesson I learned from our children's spring concert. By the end of May, Bruce had received radiation treatments to his back and his brain, and he was in the full throngs of chemotherapy treatments. Actually, he felt like crap. His heart's desire was to see Blake and Nicole's spring concert. I'm sure he secretly wondered how many more of his children's performances he would have the privilege to see.

About an hour before we needed to leave for the concert, Bruce felt nauseated and weak. He looked pale and was breaking out in cold sweats. He asked me to come into the living room, where he sat in his recliner chair. I walked up to his chair to see what was wrong. As I approached, I could tell from the anguish in his face that all was not right in his world. I fell to my knees in front of his chair and reached for his hands. With his trembling hands in mine, I knelt in silence and simply looked into his eyes. Searching for ways to make things right, I wanted his anguish to disappear. *I knew the desires of his heart, but did God?* Breaking the silence, I suggested we pray. Bruce reluctantly smiled and said, "Will you start?"

"Of course," and I started to pray.

I prayed boldly and confidently that God would overcome the power of Satan, who wanted nothing more than to keep Bruce home and keep him from seeing his children's performance. After all, if Bruce stayed home it would weaken his spirit. He would question where God was as he faced this new adversity of nausea from the chemo, radiation, and pain pills. He was so weak. Bruce added to my prayer.

"God, please give me the strength I need to go to the concert and that the nausea would hold off, at least until the concert is over."

We prayed for several minutes and then held each other's hands in silence. I stayed on my knees at the foot of his recliner and continued in my own silent prayer. Bruce had his head bowed, and his eyes were closed. I knew he was praying his own silent prayer too. Suddenly, Bruce lifted his head, opened his eyes, and said, "I'm ready . . . we need to leave now." I got up, shook out a few leg cramps, and gathered everyone in the car to leave.

Entering the school gymnasium, we found tan metal chairs set up in rows like soldiers. Luckily we came prepared and disrupted the flow by adding a blue chaise lounge chair to one of the rows. Sitting was difficult because of the cancer in Bruce's vertebrae; hard metal chairs caused unnecessary pain in his back. Because I was the school administrator, by now everyone knew of his cancer. Once he got situated, I sat next to him and began to fuss in my chair. Out of the corners of my eyes, I could see heads turn in our direction and pitifully stare. Whispers were heard, and glares bore holes in my back. People knew that Bruce had advanced cancer, yet it felt as if many treated him like he had leprosy. Some talked to me, but I almost felt like I, myself, had leprosy because I was his wife. What a terrible feeling. Some people treated us like we were fragile, like some porcelain doll that could break at the slightest touch. We needed people. We wanted them to ask, and simply to tell us they were sorry and were praying for us. That's all.

The concert was wonderful, yet I knew Bruce was not feeling well. He was being so brave. At times I found myself wishing I could take his place. It seemed more painful to watch the love of my life suffer than to actually go through it myself. The concert ended and refreshments and cookies were served. I didn't need to speculate long whether we should stay and socialize or get Bruce home. His eyes cried for home. I rounded up the family and hurried them to the car. No sooner had we arrived home and walked through the door, than Bruce made a beeline for our bedroom. I knew he was tired and wasn't up for small talk, so I followed him to make sure he was okay. What I witnessed, I will never forget.

As I entered our bedroom, I found Bruce sitting on the floor beside our bed. He was throwing up into a pail. After Bruce finished, he held the pail in front of himself and cried. I knelt down next to him and moved the pail away so I could cradle him in my arms. While holding him, tears began streaming down my face. Softly I whispered, "Honey, I am so sorry you have to go through this."

Pulling away from my embrace, Bruce looked me in the eyes and said, "Lynn, I'm not crying because I got sick . . . I'm crying because God answered my prayer. I prayed the nausea would stay away long enough so I could see the kid's concert, and God answered my prayer!"

Wow! What perspective. What faith. Bruce's reaction to his suffering on our bedroom floor that spring evening was a great testimony to me in the days to come. I realized the truth. It wasn't what our suffering looked like, but rather how we reacted and responded to our sufferings that gave us hope. This battle was definitely the Lord's, and His presence in the fight was evident.

Chapter 7

It's Never What It Seems

The Canvas

E very beautifully painted picture started out blank. The artist sees the picture long before he or she lifts a brush to begin painting. Slowly, dark and drab colors are mixed with soft pastels and bright colors. Rough lines are splashed amongst graceful strokes. Many times the artist toils and sweats painfully to create the final product.

Michelangelo hung upside down to paint the Sistine Chapel in the Vatican at Rome. It took many years to complete. What started out as a plain ceiling is now a historical and magnificent masterpiece.

From the day we are born, our lives resemble a blank canvas. Through trials, tribulations, and life experiences, we are uniquely created and transformed into the creation we were intended to be. We are a work in progress. As long as we have life, the Master Artist isn't finished with us yet. Typically, we draw our own conclusions about others from their outward appearance. Those conclusions often have inaccuracies or false judgments. People fail to recognize that those who seem to have it all may very well be carrying around a trunk full of past hardships and pain. Often, they keep them locked up from the rest of the world. Bruce's story was no different.

The Surrender

Bruce's life took many twists and turns before he arrived on the road he now traveled. Most people only saw one side of him. If you asked people to describe Bruce, they'd probably say that he was humble, a leader, strong, resilient, steady, God-fearing, brave, and confident. Those are all admirable characteristics, but many difficult situations and hard years developed these characteristics in him. It is through struggles and life experiences that our character is developed, allowing us to deal with what life might throw our way. I thank God that He loved Bruce so much that He didn't leave him where he was at when I first met him.

Bruce's past life was different from what most people now viewed. They didn't know the strongholds that affected him. Like young David in the Bible, God had been preparing Bruce for the grand finale; we just weren't aware of it at the time.

People loved Bruce, but Bruce didn't always like Bruce. He didn't walk closely with his Lord in his early years, but that was because he didn't know his Lord personally. I remember studying one Sunday in my dorm room at SCSU. I was sitting at my desk, and he sat on the couch studying for a test. The room was quiet until, out of the blue, he said to me, "You're a Christian, aren't you?" I was surprised by this question, because he and I had never talked about church, faith, or anything that would bring about this question. I turned in my chair to face him.

"Yes, why do you ask, and how did you know that?"

He looked at me and said, "I just knew."

I just knew? How? I thought.

He proceeded to explain that he thought everyone who called themselves "Christians" were living in some kind of a Coca-Cola commercial. They had no grasp on reality and were basically living in a fantasy world.

"You're different," Bruce said. He knew that something was missing in his life, but he wasn't sure what it was. I guess that somehow my silence spoke volumes. Learning a great lesson that day, I realized I have two choices—I can either talk the talk or walk the walk. At that moment, I recognized I chose to walk the walk. Bruce saw and heard despite my silence.

After Bruce's unusual question, we talked about his faith or lack of faith as he called it. He believed there was a God in the logical and intellectual sense, but he had never asked Jesus Christ into his heart to be his Lord and Savior. He never experienced what it was like to be completely in love with the Lord, even with his imperfections. He had never felt that yearning of wanting to serve God. He was searching to fill a hole in his soul. During most of his college years, he experimented with various drugs, alcohol, and whatever filled the void he felt. Don't misunderstand me—Bruce was well liked by everyone he met; he had many close friends and a great family. But despite his outward appearance, Bruce was inwardly choking.

Bruce's love for me was apparent, and my love for him was equally strong. God had placed upon my heart early on that Bruce would be the one I'd marry some day. The only thing that bothered me was the disjointedness of our faith. I had a child-like faith. Bruce was searching and questioning his own.

Ever since I was a little girl, Jesus was my best friend. I love the famous painting of Jesus surrounded by children and holding one in his arms. When I am sad, I envision myself as that lone child on Jesus' lap.

Like other young girls, I dreamed of a fairy tale romance. You know the one—the knight in shining armor that comes to rescue the distressed princess. The prince would kiss her, and they'd live happily ever after. I dreamed of someone like that. I even saw that prince as one I could share my childlike faith in God with. That Sunday I learned that Bruce's faith was very different than mine, and yet God was leading me to him.

I loved him so much, and I needed to trust in God's greater plan.

I recall another time when Bruce came to see me at my efficiency apartment. College graduation came and went, and I had moved back to St. Cloud after living in the Twin Cities. When he arrived I could tell he had been drinking heavily. I was mad and sad at the same time. We had been apart, and by now we were planning our wedding. *He had to drink to see me? The nerve!* I felt jilted. I suspected for some time that Bruce might have a problem with alcohol abuse. Later that evening, I couldn't help but confront him. After questioning him on his drinking and asking all the "whys," Bruce started to cry. He fell to his knees. I felt bad for him, and it was as if I could see the torment stirring within him. He said, "I don't want to be like this, Lynn, but I don't know how to get beyond this."

I knelt beside him and asked, "Is it okay to pray for you?"

"Please."

I'll never forget closing my eyes that evening. As I was praying for Bruce, it was as if I saw a battle being waged between good and evil. I grabbed Bruce's hand and told him what I saw. He began to cry harder. He said what I saw described exactly how he felt. He felt a constant tug between good and evil, and he was caught in the middle.

"What do you want, Bruce?" I asked.

"I want Jesus in my life. I'm tired of the fight. I can't do this on my own anymore. I'm ready to surrender." With his hand in mine and his tears anointing them, I asked God to come fill Bruce. I asked God to show him how much He loved him and how much God wants to be a part of his life in a personal way. He then asked that Jesus come into his heart and heal him. I remember him saying, "I don't even know what to ask for Lord, but I know you know what I need. Please help me." It was such a simple prayer, and yet that moment was the second pivotal point in our relationship. It was like a new breath of life flooded into Bruce. He still struggled with his drinking. Eventually, we were married and moved to Brainerd, Minnesota. Not long after, we crossed another "make or break" point. Thankfully, he chose the "make" point.

The Sobriety

Three weeks and three days into our marriage, Bruce came home very late one night. He had been drinking again. His car had broken down just blocks from our apartment, and a cop pulled over to help him out. The policeman could tell that he'd had too much to drink. People tended to know who's who in small town Brainerd, and the policeman was no exception. Realizing who Bruce was and the role he held in the community, he proceeded to lecture him up one side and down the other. Bruce worked professionally for the Boy Scouts—what kind of message was he sending by drinking and driving? The policeman also knew that Bruce was newly married. What kind of message was he sending to his wife coming home at 2:00 in the morning? Thankfully, the policeman didn't give him a citation. He told Bruce that he knew the chastisement he'd receive from his new bride would be punishment enough. Little did Bruce know, he had just been given a "get out of jail free" card. Once again, God was protecting him for a greater purpose.

Abandoning our car in the ditch with a broken tie rod, the policeman dropped him off at our apartment. Feeling humiliated, Bruce left the squad car like a scared dog with his tail between his legs. He was about to enter the third pivotal point in our relationship. I was worried sick. It was late, and my thoughts went to ditches and hospitals. How dare he put me through this! I was furious when I learned that a policeman brought him home after he was out having his own pity party. Bruce had lied to me about why he was late. He drove up to the cabin with beer, lots of it, and proceeded to drink alone. The funny thing was, he had given his life over to Christ. But he clung to the one comfort that he wasn't ready to relinquish—alcohol. I didn't sleep much that night. At 6 A.M., I finally got up to unpack the final boxes from the move into our new apartment.

"I refuse to be a part of this," I cried as I threw a shoe across the room. "I will not be a part of your lying and childish actions. When we took our marriage vows, it was for better or for worse and till death do us part. You're stuck with me, but I refuse to live like this!"

That morning, silent fear exuded from our bedroom where Bruce lay. From that day forth, Bruce prayed that God would carry him and remove this stronghold from him. He knew there was nothing in his power to get him through the desire for alcohol and asked God to carry him. Sound familiar? He went to see a Christian psychologist he knew at the Brainerd hospital. The psychologist told him it was only by the grace of God that he caught his alcohol abuse so early. Bruce attended many AA meetings, and I went to a few Alanon meetings. Eventually Bruce stopped attending AA meetings. He no longer had someone to hold him accountable.

"Lynn, I don't need these meetings anymore. God is carrying me through this, and *He* is holding me accountable." Somehow I believed him and knew in my heart that God was far bigger and more powerful than any urge for alcohol. He was stronger than any tormenting thoughts to drink that slithered back into his mind. *Thank you, God, for going after your lost sheep, even though Bruce wandered for years without You being his Shepherd.* He never had a drop of alcohol or any drugs since the summer of 1986. This period of "letting go and letting God take over" freed him. God never let Bruce down, even during the remaining 16 ½ years of his young life. Praise God for his sobriety and for God's faithfulness!

With the help of God, Bruce lived on victoriously, but he never was void of temptations. He would have times of doubts, unworthiness, and feelings of defeat, none of which were of God. God had called him to do great things. He had to lean on the very One who created him to fight the new battles before him. Thankfully, it no longer was a fight he had to fight alone.

The One Desire

Once Bruce gave his life completely over to Christ, it became like a construction phase in motion, building a lifelong legacy. Ephesians 2:10 says, "For we are God's workmanship, created in Christ Jesus to do good works, which God prepared in advance for us to do." Bruce's one desire was to be obedient and to do God's will for his life. To accomplish all God required, whether he understood it or not. Passion and conviction followed Bruce wherever he went. He was on fire for his Lord, and others around him could feel it.

Bruce wanted to minister to all who God placed before him. Two qualities I found so precious in Bruce were his ability to be uninhibited by the reaction of others toward him and his incredible sense of urgency to get things done. I now understand why. He loved people, but he loved the Lord even more.

Bruce went to his first Promise Keepers weekend in Boulder, Colorado, in 1994. He rode in a big van with twelve other guys. They called themselves the Bakers Dozen. It was a beautiful point in his relationship with God and other Christian men. His good friend Paul Froland went with him. After that weekend, promises were made, prayers were lifted, and Bible studies began. Out of that first Promise Keepers gathering, Paul and Bruce felt lead to create a local men's group called *Trinity Iron Men,* which eventually evolved into *Men of Faith.* Their desire was to call, unite, and strengthen the local men of our community, from all denominations and walks of life, to *grow up* in God and in His calling. They saw the need for men to step out as Christian men in today's society and stand for what was good and right. The *Trinity Iron Men* and *Men of Faith* movement was just one of the burning desires that Bruce felt led to ignite for the cause of Christ.

In 1997, the Lord placed upon Bruce's heart the vision and mission of building a new area-wide Lutheran school that would encompass many churches. It included community outreach and would reach out to families that are hurting and have services the church could support. The church we attended had a school, but it was old and needed a lot of repairs and updates. The best alternative was to construct a new building. Bruce often told me, "No one in their right mind would take on such a monumental task. I'm trying to create a new school with six congregations. Trying to get one congregation to decide on the color of carpet is next to impossible in most churches . . . and I'm asking them to agree on building a new community school?"

After three years of research, hard work, and long hours, the task force seemed to have the support of all the congregations. By the grace of God, six congregations unanimously voted to join forces to build the new school. It officially had the congregation's ownership, now it needed to be incorporated with the State of Minnesota.

In the summer of 2000, Bruce anxiously entered our State Capitol. The entire task force had worked so hard, and he was now ready to officially consecrate something that had taken years to develop. He said the paper work took just minutes. He presented the appropriate check, a few stamps and signatures were added to the document, and he was handed the official incorporation statement. It was done. Final. On that beautiful summer afternoon, Bruce walked out of the state office and found himself suddenly engulfed with deep emotions. The Capitol steps were grand, and he managed to get halfway down them before he collapsed. With one hand on the railing and the other hand covering his face, he sat in broad daylight and wept. Emotions flooded over him like water over a dam. The presence of God was evident, intense and powerful.

"It felt like God, Himself, was sitting on those Capitol steps right next to me," Bruce said. At that moment, I believe he was on holy ground. Psalm 16:11 says, "You have made known to me the path of life; you will fill me with joy in your presence, with eternal pleasures at your right hand."

Bruce now knew that no matter what mountains lay before him, God was bigger. The new school was God's will, and Bruce knew that God would see it through to completion. Philippians 1:6 reads, "Being confident of this, that he who began a good work in you will carry it on to completion until the day of Christ Jesus." I've never seen Bruce so excited about anything before. It was clear to me that he actually experienced the presence and power of God sitting right next to him that warm summer day. Many of us are lucky enough to experience seeing the hand of God in indirect ways, but few of us are blessed like Bruce was to feel His presence in a real and direct way. He was one with God in his spirit and soul.

Bruce's one desire was to be obedient to God's calling. He didn't always understand and he often doubted, but he learned through experience to have faith in the unseen and to trust in God's calling. Faith was the one requirement. Witnessing what Bruce was able to accomplish taught me that God doesn't always call the equipped, but He always will equip the called!

Chapter 8

Outwardly Wasting Away

The Alarm Clock

As each day presented itself to us, our platter was filled with something unique. One particular Saturday was no different.

I've always used the snooze button on our alarm clock for different reasons than what the manufacturer intended. Every morning I find myself pressing the snooze button three times for reasons other than snoozing. It started when our two children were very small. Like every other mother, I found myself feeling that once my feet hit the floor in the morning, my time would not be my own until the children were neatly tucked into their beds at night and fast asleep. It was then that I'd have *my* time. Ha! Right. It usually never happened, because I was exhausted by the time the kids were dreaming sweet dreams and I had the house picked up after busy days. All I wanted to do was crawl in bed and go to sleep. The frustrating thing about this routine was that I missed my time with God that I so desperately needed. I wanted to start the day out on the right foot, with the right heart.

One Saturday morning, several years back, Nicole gently tip-toed into my room and marched right up beside my bed. Blake followed. The alarm clock had awakened me only moments earlier, but my eyelids were not cooperating. As Nicole approached the bed, I heard her softly whisper, "Mommy? Are you 'wake?" By this time I discovered that not only were my eyelids not cooperating, but also my mouth refused to work, and my muscles acted like they were paralyzed! It was as if my body parts were all going on strike. I never answered her. There was a pause in the room, and then I heard her small voice say, "Bakey, shhhh, Mommy's 'till seepin." Before I could respond, they tiptoed back out of the room, in the same fashion they entered.

Ahhh . . . quiet.

Then God spoke to me and said. *OK . . . now talk to me.*

Not sleep? I asked.

No, talk to me.

OK, I thought, so I did. I started to pray, and I found myself pouring out my heart to the very One I had longed to spend time with in the days prior. I wasn't done talking to God when suddenly the alarm buzzer started to ring again. I reached across the bed and hit the snooze button one more time. What a wonderful morning it was turning out to be, and my feet hadn't even hit the floor yet. I continued my morning prayer until the alarm went off one last time, then I got up for the day. From that morning forward, I've used the alarm clock to wake me up so I could begin my day in conversation with God. My days seem to go better. To this day, my children still think that when I'm in bed and my eyes are closed, I'm sleeping. Little do they know I'm probably praying.

After years of waking up to the alarm clock and spending time with God, this one particular day would be no different. The day ahead of us would be filled with new experiences and a new awareness of God's detail and love. It was on this particular Saturday that hair cuts and hair clippers would take on a whole new meaning; a day when a strand of hair would signify a strand of time in God's big picture.

The Clippers

Continuing in the tradition of beginning my days in quiet conversation with God, I now ended my days in prayer each night until I fell asleep. It was almost as if my body associated the closing of my eyes in bed as a time of worship. It became a time I would spend in the arms of my heavenly Father. My soul was still and I could listen, a luxury the busyness of the day didn't seem to provide.

One night after Bruce had received several rounds of chemo, I found myself reflecting on the day that was nearly over. Alone with God, I told Him that Bruce had started to lose his hair that day—a lot of hair. Early that morning Bruce had reached up to scratch his head, and when he pulled his hand away, a fist full of hair was in his hand. In disbelief, he put his hand up to his head again and tried to pull on his hair. This time even more hair lay between his fingers. This was a day we both knew would come, yet neither was prepared for it. The chemo had done this. It was ultimately another reminder of how this uninvited cold and calculating cancer had invaded his body and created havoc.

I was to meet Jim Stigman, a friend of ours, that morning. We were scheduled to go to a greenhouse to pick out flowers and plants for my gardens. Before I even had a chance to shower, Bruce informed me that it was time to get out the clippers. I knew what that meant. He sat on a chair in the kitchen. I draped him with the same brown cape I've used for the past eighteen years to cut his hair. As I turned on the clippers, they sounded so loud and terrible. Today the clippers seemed to growl in my hands. Nevertheless, it was time. I chose the largest teeth to put on the clippers so the cut would not be such a shock to Bruce. He had such pretty and thick dark brown hair, with a slight wave to it. I told Bruce to put his chin down and proceeded to move the clippers up the back side of his head.

I had gotten halfway up the backside when he yelled, "Stop." Startled, I immediately stopped.

"That's fine, Bruce, but I think it's too late. People will really notice it if I just leave your hair this way," I jokingly teased.

"No, that's not it. We forgot to pray."

Pray? Now?

I was stunned by his response. My dear husband, with tear filled eyes, began to pray to our loving Father about the loss of his hair. In humbleness he asked God to give him peace and strength. Finishing his prayer, he announced, "OK, you can finish now."

The hair cut went from the largest clipper length to the medium clipper length, then finally to the smallest clipper length. It was the shortest I'd ever seen Bruce's hair, but he looked good. Johnny Verkennes, the best man in our wedding, came over just when I was about to finish. He even took a picture of the work of art. When Nicole came home from the neighbors, she hugged her Daddy and told him that he was the "handsomest Daddy" in the whole wide world. The kids loved the short, short hair cut. Bruce just smiled.

In our kitchen that ordinary Saturday morning, with a brown cape wrapped around Bruce's neck and clippers in my hand, God, in his grace, answered the smallest of prayers from one of his hurting children. God knows every hair on our heads. Matthew 10:30 reads, "And even the very hairs of your head are all numbered." I would imagine that God also knows every hair that falls from our heads too. I found myself asking God to bless Bruce that night and in all the days to come. Silently I prayed, "Give Bruce peace in knowing that it's what's on the inside that makes the man. It's what's 'in the head' that makes him wise. It's what's in his heart that makes him strong, and it's your permanent mark on him that makes him yours." I rolled over and said, "Good night, Bruce, angels on your pillow."

Then I fell asleep.

The Lunch Date

Summer was here. Father's Day was soon approaching, and major decisions needed to be made. Bruce was showing outward signs of the ravages from the cancer. He had dropped about twenty pounds. His clothes sagged on him. Hair had fallen out in blotches and left obvious bald patches all over his head. Even though it was shaved down to virtually nothing, it appeared odd and abnormal. His face was thin and gaunt. Sensitive eyes watered and appeared blistery. Burnt spots bellowed by his temple and neck area from the radiation to his head. When he didn't know I was looking, I'd sneak glimpses of him and just want to cry.

One day for lunch, we decided to go to the *Old Country Buffet*. We went there because Bruce never knew what he could or couldn't eat. It was a game he hadn't mastered. Being able to try a variety of foods seemed to be the best way to know what he could tolerate on that particular day. Near the end of May, the weather was sunny and warm. Bruce looked out of place because he wore a lightweight sweater; he was always cold. After we finished eating, the manager came up to our booth and said, "I hope you ladies enjoyed your lunch."

We looked dumbfounded at each other, and I managed to mumble out a "Yes."

When the manager left, Bruce looked at me, paused, and said, "Did he just say what I think he did?" Neither of us could believe it. We just sat there and laughed. I felt bad for Bruce. Outwardly he was looking different, but inwardly he was the handsome man I fell in love with. On the way home he quoted from 2 Corinthians 4:16, saying, "'Therefore we do not lose heart. Though outwardly we are wasting away, yet inwardly we are being renewed day by day.' This verse has given me great comfort these past few weeks." When I arrived home, I pulled out my Bible and looked up that verse. Bruce was right. What great comfort.

I read on to verse 17 and 18. "For our light and momentary troubles are achieving for us an eternal glory that far outweighs them all. So we fix our eyes not on what is seen, but on what is unseen. For what is seen is temporary, but what is unseen is eternal." That gave me peace. Reflecting on lunch that day, I thought of how God looks at us and sees us. Whether we like it or not, He sees us from the "inside out", and He knows exactly who we are, despite our outward appearance. The image of God seeing us from the "inside out" wouldn't leave my mind. Later that evening, I pulled out an old poetry book I started in high school. One of the poems I had written reflected the thoughts of that day. It was a child's view of how God loves us from the "inside out."

Ode to MISTER GOD

There's a great many things about Mister God that we don't know about, and if we don't know many things about Mister God, how do we know He loves us?

Mister God doesn't love us. He doesn't really.
You know, only people can love. I can love you
and you can love me because you are a people.
I love Mister God truly, but He doesn't love me.
No, no, He doesn't love me.
Not like you do, it's different.
Its millions of trillion times bigger.
Mister God is different.

People can only love outside and kiss outside, but
Mister God can love you right inside,
and Mister God can kiss you right inside, so it's different.
Mister God is different from us because He can finish things
and we can't. I can't finish loving you, because I shall die

millions of years before I can finish loving you,
so it's not the same kind of love.

Even Mister Jesus' love isn't the same as Mister God's
because He only came here to make us remember.
He was our teacher and our Savior.
Because we were bad, he came to take our place
so we can all be together some day with
Mister God in heaven.

Mister Jesus sacrificed the best, He sacrificed Himself.

Everybody has got a point of view, but Mister God hasn't.
Mister God has only points to view. And Mister God can
know things and people from the inside of them.
We only know them from the outside, don't we?
So you see, people can't talk about Mister God from the
outside; you can only talk about Mister God
from the inside of Him.

So now that I've told you some things about Mister God,
love him, OK?
He's my best friend. Treat Him special.

Kiss the air,—He's there
He'll kiss you back—right on your inside!

Lynn

What a simplistic way I viewed God when I was young. I
now desired that child-like faith to take over my adult life
and become my autopilot. It was through writing when I was
young that I expressed myself, and it continued throughout
my adulthood. Maybe that's why the e-mails were such a

wonderful tool to talk to the masses. Maybe that's why journaling seemed to keep me afloat when I felt like I was drowning. It was the life jacket I could strap on at any time. The simple task of journaling became a saving grace in many ways. I was able to express myself with things that were so private that only my pen and the paper would be privy to. Even on lunch dates when my husband was seen as someone totally different from who he was, I was comforted in knowing that God sees us for who we really are. By now, my world had shattered into tiny little pieces. It was "Mister God" who was the glue holding all the pieces together, even the smallest of slivers. Praise God for meeting us right where we're at. Right in our insides—shattered pieces and all.

The Air Conditioning Unit

June was here and summer was in full swing. Our families were wonderful. They traveled from Minnesota, Wisconsin, Iowa, and Louisiana. Even though they were devastated by the course of events, they wasted no time doing what they could to help.

Bruce had finished a series of fifteen radiation treatments to his spine and was half way through the series of fifteen radiation treatments to his brain. He continued with his weekly chemo treatments and was really suffering from the combined effects of everything. When Bruce hurt, I hurt; when he felt good, I felt good. We traveled together . . . we fought together . . . we lived and laughed together . . . and we spent countless hours together in prayer. I began to tape every card that was sent to us on our walls. It was a great reminder of all the love and support we were receiving from others. The notes and Scripture verses in the cards continued to give us strength and hope. It became our new wallpaper.

Bruce's brother, Chuck, and his family came from Baton Rouge, Louisiana. As soon as they arrived they pitched right in. They completed projects around the house and yard work. It was great having them here. My brothers, Dean and Dale, Paul, a friend of Dean's, and my brother-in-law, John, came and ripped out our old deck on the back of the house, then built a new one for us, which was bigger and better. The labor of love we saw during those summer months was next to amazing and so appreciated. Bruce was so excited when we finally got air conditioning. With one of his lungs almost completely collapsed, breathing was a new challenge. Humidity in the Minnesota summers can be almost unbearable for healthy lungs, let alone compressed lungs. Once it was installed, he breathed much more easily.

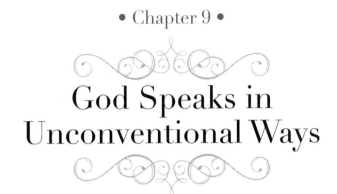

God Speaks in Unconventional Ways

The Frog

Years ago I gave my friend Jennifer a cute, little stuffed frog. Sound funny? Well, the reason I gave her the frog wasn't funny to her. Ever since meeting her I've known she was deathly afraid of dentists. I'm not sure of the underlying reason for this paralyzing fear, but I knew how real it was to her. Even the word "dentist" sent chills up her spine.

One day we decided to have lunch. During lunch, the extent of her fear was evident. The next week Jennifer needed to go to the dentist, and she was worried. It wasn't for a regular check up either. She needed a root canal. I've never had a root canal, but I've heard it can be a terrible experience and dreaded event. Just the sound of it makes me cringe. Nothing I could say to her would take away her fear and anxiety during lunch. We talked about praying before the appointment, giving it to God, and many other ways to curb her fear. It's funny how all the "shoulds" in life simply fall short of giving us comfort when we need it the most.

I offered to go with Jennifer to the appointment and give her moral support. I'm not sure what good I would have done. I envisioned myself holding her hand while the dentist had his hand in her mouth, all the while asking her what she was up to these days and if she had taken any trips lately.

Why do they do that? They ask you questions with suction hoses, gauze, and their fist in your mouth! Then they expect you to answer them. What's up with that? Do dentists take classes on interpreting things like, "Ah, I ent u orthhh oo ishhh enn aut ah ig unn"? (The English translation is "Ah, I went up north to fish and caught a big one!") In doing so, don't they get tired of getting showered with spit? Maybe they later e-mail their counterparts to see who can out do the other with the best gibberish stories. I think they should just give you massive amounts of laughing gas and stick head phones over your ears with blaring music to cover up the sounds of their nasty tools like drills, picks, and those sharp scrapy things.

Jennifer bravely told me that she'd go to the appointment alone. She needed to face this fear. In my prayer time I asked God to show me if there was anything I could do to alleviate her anxiety. Then it came to me. My teeny beanie baby frog! I'd give it to her to put in her pocket, and she could pull it out during the procedure. It was small enough to be concealed, yet big enough in symbolism to make her strong.

I was going to see her before her appointment, so I wrote out a card explaining the frog to her. I gently wrapped the frog in tissue paper and put him in a gift bag. I explained that FROG stood for *Fully Rely On God*. She was to put the little green frog in her pocket and then when lying in the dental chair, take it out and hold it. It would remind her to *fully rely on God* during her appointment. Her focus would be on God, and she would know that with God all things are possible—even surviving a root canal! Jennifer appreciated the gift and was excited to take the frog along with her. She called me after her appointment and couldn't believe how much the frog helped her. She pulled it out of her pocket, held it, and gently rubbed it the entire time. Her thoughts went to God, His power, might, and soothing comfort. What a help! She had several follow up appointments and was no longer afraid. She wasn't looking forward to the appointments, but the paralyzing fear that she once experienced seemed to melt away. Each time, the frog hopped along with her to the appointments.

Time went by, and Jennifer had a friend whose husband had just lost his job. Money was tight. They had four small children to feed, and the unknown future was scary. The paralyzing fear they were feeling crept into their thoughts, and they asked themselves where God was when jobs and paychecks are lost. What did Jennifer do? She took the teeny beanie frog and gave it to her friend as a reminder to always *Fully Rely On God*. Before they knew it, the friend's husband landed another job. Better than the last. The frog didn't find the job, but he was a reminder of who really was in control.

Years had passed since I saw that cute little frog, but I never forgot about him. In fact, every time I see a frog of any type, I'm always reminded to fully rely on God. I smile when I think of God's sense of humor. What a funny little creature to help focus us on our Life Maker instead of a situation that seems to be our life destroyer.

Cancer had become a life destroyer for Bruce and me. My eyes were struggling to see anything worth viewing. Then, one day after my Bible study fellowship class, Jennifer asked me to come over to her car. She presented me with a gift bag and a card. The gift was a tiny beanie frog. Could this be the same frog from several years ago? The note read that Jennifer had to search to find the frog. Just about the time her friend was going to give it to someone else, Jennifer intercepted it. And yes, this was the same little frog from several years ago. She knew Bruce and I could use the frog now. I cried at her kind gesture. I needed to refocus on God and rely on His mighty power. Like "bifocals" I needed "Godfocals." The frog focused us on what really mattered, and it would eventually prove to be a much larger ministry that touched many. We took that frog everywhere with us. It went to every doctor visit and chemo appointment. It even rode on Bruce's chest for every medical test.

Many people asked about our cute, little, green friend, and Bruce radiated with God's love at every inquiry, because he could once again tell the story of what it meant to *Fully Rely On God!* Not only was our frog a reminder of someone much bigger than we are, but also it taught us that God can speak to us in many different ways. Often times—unconventionally.

The Waiting Room Angel

Have you been graced by the presence of an angel? Have you seen an angel in the flesh or met one in person and spoken to one? Have you ever thought you might have, but you weren't sure? I believe I have. An angel is a spiritual being, a messenger or minister of God. Hebrews 1:14 says, "Are not all angels ministering spirits sent to serve those who will inherit salvation?" Again in Hebrews, Paul was talking to the persecuted Christian Jews who needed encouragement. Hebrews 13:2 reads, "Do not forget to entertain strangers, for by so doing some people have entertained angels without knowing it." Why is it that we question instead of trust when someone we don't know comes into our life, often at the very moment we need them? Many times the encounters we have with strangers have an ultimate purpose. Let me give you a perfect example.

The fluids around Bruce's lungs were building up to a level that made him extremely uncomfortable. Even eating was a challenge. He took a few bites and could take no more. Talking was exhausting, because he was unable to expand his lungs to accommodate the appropriate air he needed to carry on a conversation. The pressure from the fluid build up was preventing the basic necessities for life—eating and breathing.

Bruce's 40th birthday was soon approaching and so was Father's Day. We had to wonder: with all of the prayers of the Prayer Warriors, where was the relief? We sent the kids with their cousins up to the family cabin over Father's Day weekend. Bruce would be "in the valley" before this special weekend, and all he desired was a quiet house.

We called his oncologist and asked for an immediate appointment with a pulmonologist to get the fluid from his chest wall drained off. As Bruce told the doctor, "If I don't get it drained soon, I don't think I'll make it through the weekend." The doctor knew Bruce was in dire straits. Bruce had seen him several days before, and you could hear the struggle in his labored voice. Within several hours we received a call back. It was the appointment we had hoped for. A pulmonologist could see Bruce the next day at the hospital.

The handicapped parking tag we now carried in the car was turning out to be a Godsend. Bruce labored just to walk to the admitting area of the hospital. He walked slowly and methodically. After he was admitted, a wheelchair was provided. Whew!

Bruce's lungs had only been drained once before. I accompanied him when the first fluid was taken, so I never questioned whether I should be in the room with him this time. The pulmonologist still asked me if I wanted to remain in the room while the procedure was performed.

"Of course," I said, "I was with Bruce during the last procedure, and I'm not about to leave him now."

But Bruce was at a different place this time than the first. In the last five weeks his body had been through a war zone, and he was showing the battle scars. The procedure room was larger and far more sterile than the quaint little office of the first fluid extraction. There was nothing welcoming about this room. Looking at all the grey metal gave me chills and made me shudder. Bruce sat sideways on the middle of the bed, with his feet dangling down. He wore a hospital gown, with the opening to the back. He was told to lean over the metal tray in front of him as if he was hugging it, and the doctor would begin. Bruce cringed and even jumped as he touched the tray. "Can I have a pillow on the tray to cushion the blow?" he asked in disgust.

Why didn't they think of that?

I was a little perturbed. He even had to ask for some ice water. The radiation and chemo left him parched all the time. Bruce was given water, along with a flimsy pillow. Now the procedure could begin. I was happy for him and actually looked forward to the thoracentesis. I knew Bruce would get relief from the fluid extraction. I was even glad to be in this unwelcome and sterile room, because I knew Bruce would leave here feeling better than when he arrived.

When the procedure began, a long needle was inserted into Bruce's back to the pleural space between his chest wall and lungs. A long tube connected the needle to a two-liter bottle, and the fluid that was extracted drained into the bottle. I laughed to myself, because there was no reason why they needed to hook up such a large bottle, but *oh, well* I thought.

Suddenly, my mind went into shock. My eyes saw the bottle filling up very fast with a dark red fluid.

Am I really seeing what I think I'm seeing? I thought in horror.

Then my chest ached, as if my own blood was being flushed right out of my body. My head was getting light, and I knew that if I didn't leave the room soon, I'd be face down on the floor in no time. Forcing my weak legs to stand up, I proceeded to the door. As I left the room, I was aghast to see that they were hooking up a second bottle!

My God, I'm going to pass out. Hold me up!

As I opened the door, I heard Bruce gasp for air and moan in pain. He never did that the first time. It tore at my heart. Once in the hallway, I braced myself against the wall.

My God, was that really blood I saw pouring into that bottle? Please be with Bruce. I saw a nurse in the hallway. With a trembling voice, I asked her if I could have a glass of water.

"Where's your husband's glass?"

Surprised by that question, I replied, "No, that would be for me."

Seeing I was pale, she quickly brought me a small styrofoam cup of water. Then she pointed me in the direction of the nearest waiting room. I left my purse and shoulder bag in the procedure room. I didn't care. I needed to get away. I needed air. When I walked into the small waiting room, I found myself alone, or so I thought. I was wearing a red T-shirt underneath a denim shirt. I faced the wall and began peeling off my denim shirt. I needed to breathe. It was hot. My palms were cold and clammy. My heart beat rapidly. Tears welled up in my eyes, and my throat was closing. I wanted to scream.

Unexpectedly, I felt a presence. Looking over my shoulder, I saw a woman. I hadn't noticed her when I first arrived in the room. She had a clipboard in her hand and was filling out a form. The hospital band affixed to her right wrist indicated she must have been there for a procedure. Her hair was short and a beautiful grey. She must have been in her early 60s. Then an inner voice spoke to me.

Speak to this woman.

I remember so distinctly looking up at the ceiling tiles and answering back in my head, *I don't think so!* Frankly, I was annoyed those words even came to me. Then I had the audacity to think, *Excuse me . . . can't you see that I'm having a little breakdown here and a little help would be nice?*

What nerve I had. After all, I knew exactly *who* I was talking to. Then I turned around again to look at the woman who I was supposed to talk to. *Ha,* I thought. *What an absurd thought. Oh no, she looked at me.*

Our eyes made contact. I turned away.

Then the voice came a second time; *you need to speak with this woman.*

For crying out loud, I defiantly thought. Only then, I did. A small portion of the dam that was holding back those swelling tears cracked. I grabbed a tissue from the Kleenex box to conceal my tears, and I sat on a chair across the room from the woman. A third time, the voice spoke to me and by now, this woman was looking directly at me. She didn't say a word. Wiping away my tears as inconspicuously as I could, I heard myself say, "So, why are you here?"

Now that was a novel question, Lynn. Good job! I thought. *Shut up,* I told myself. *I'm just being obedient.*

The mysterious woman commented she was there to get an MRI of her brain. A pregnant pause ensued.

Taunting me again, an inner voice said, *OK, smarty, now what do you say?* Ignoring the voice, I responded, "I'm sorry, are you having headaches?"

My inner voice was just about to mock me again and say, *Brilliant response, Lynn . . .* when the women proceeded to tell me what transpired for her to be there that day. I actually don't remember much about what she said. That is until she asked, "So, why are you here?"

The crack in the dam gave way. Through my tears, I started telling her the reason—my husband was having a thoracentesis because he had fluid around his lungs from cancer. By now the woman was crying too, so I grabbed the box of Kleenex and went over to sit beside her. She told me she knew exactly how I felt, because she had lost her husband four years ago from lung cancer. He had several thoracentesis too. Amazing! We talked, we cried, and we shared stories. She held me up when I was too weak to stand. She encouraged me in the Lord, and she told me never to apologize for my tears, anger, and sadness.

"The Lord wants to hear about the pains of your heart," she said, "no matter how it comes out." She asked if we had children. "You need to be strong for them. That's what God is for," she said. "He's got big shoulders, and He can take whatever, you throw at him. Besides He knows what is in our hearts—He knows everything!"

Time flew. Eventually, a friend of ours who worked in the radiation department brought my purse and shoulder bag to the waiting room. She told me Bruce would be coming out shortly. My new friend and I exchanged names and phone numbers. Her name was Corrine, and she told me to call her anytime of the day or night! I'm embarrassed to admit that my thoughts were, *Sure, that's what they all say and then they lose your phone number.* Not only did Corrine *not* lose my phone number, but also she called me every week in the long days ahead. We became good friends.

As I stood to leave, she stood up too and gave me a much-needed hug. Then she grabbed my shoulders, looked me straight in my tear filled eyes, and said, "Be strong in the Lord and know that I *will call you.*" Wow! What I would have missed if I hadn't listened to the voice of God that afternoon. Maybe it was the Holy Spirit whispering in my ear, but nonetheless, I knew it was God ordained. I learned a long time ago that it is not my place to question, but rather to obey—even when it just doesn't make sense. What a lesson I learned that afternoon. God knew what I needed even when I didn't. I just needed to trust in that still, small voice. I also learned that God is a God of second and third chances, even when I didn't deserve it. I couldn't wait to tell Bruce about my encounter with my new friend, Corrine. I began to fondly call her my "waiting room angel." Bruce was feeling better after the procedure, and

I could tell that he was happy for me and my "waiting room angel" experience.

When we arrived home, Bruce was tired and ready for a nap. He immediately went to his recliner, kicked up the footrest, and pulled his favorite fleece blanket tightly under his chin. Before he fell asleep, I told him how scared I was that morning when I saw all the blood they were extracting from around his lungs. After listening to my story, he looked at me, smiled, and said, "I guess you can say that I'm covered in Christ's blood."

Then he closed his eyes and fell asleep.

The God Zone

Even during the blazing heat of June, Bruce stayed comfortable in our home with our newly installed air conditioning. However, it was the humidity that affected him more than the heat. Knowing our children were up at the cabin with their cousins eased our minds. They needed to be "kids," and the house could be quiet while Bruce was "in the valley" after another chemo treatment. "In the valley" was now the common expression we used after he went through each chemo treatment. The first twenty-four hours were not that bad, but from the second through sixth day, he felt awful. The doctors usually gave him a shot that would increase his white blood cell count. Unfortunately, one of the side effects of this procedure was flu-like symptoms. On top of the side effects of the chemo and a sensitive stomach, Bruce's joints would ache.

During those "valley walking" days, it was my job to care for Bruce and keep the house as quiet as possible. He usually wrapped himself in his fleece blanket, lay in the fetal position, and watched TV or slept. It was a joy and privilege to love and serve my husband in such a selfless way—no matter what he looked like or how he felt.

Father's Day was near, and the entire MacKenzie clan was at the family cabin. Bruce was very weak but knew how important it was to make every effort to join the family. After several days of resting at home and getting the thoracentesis, he started feeling better. He breathed and ate more easily. We decided to trust God for continued restoration and set out for the two-hour trip to the cabin. Everyone was so excited that he could join them. Physically, he was spiraling down hill quickly and wasn't responding to the chemo treatments as we had hoped. We weren't sure if this would be the last Father's Day he would spend with his own Father, and our two children needed desperately to spend this day with their dad.

The day was great. He opened gifts, and we took pictures and videos. Bruce was tired, but he hung in there. The weekend turned out to be very eventful. It was not only Father's Day, but also a big decision was made, a priceless memory created, and an unusual event witnessed by the entire family.

One of the decisions we needed to make that weekend was whether or not we should find a new cancer treatment facility. The current center had basically thrown in the towel on Bruce, and we were going nowhere fast. We were told that if he was lucky, he might have two months left to live. They wanted to send him home and give him palliative care. Meaning, they offered to send him home with medications to curb the pain. We needed a "Plan B."

After a lot of research on other options, discussions, list making of pros and cons, phone calls, and prayer, we finally narrowed it down to two different cancer treatment centers where we could go next. When it came time to actually make the big decision, Bruce grabbed my hand and led me into the corner bedroom where we usually stayed. There we could be alone. With both of us on our knees beside the bed, he tightly held my hands. In heartfelt prayer we asked for God's guidance and wisdom. When we had finished I opened my eyes and looked at Bruce. He seemed to have a smile on his face, and he said, "Well, do you know where we need to go? I do."

Confidently smiling back at him I said, "Yes, I do too . . . but you go first."

In Bruce's typical style he said, "No, you go—ladies first."

I laughed and told him it was Parker Hughes Cancer Treatment Center in Minneapolis/St. Paul area.

Bruce immediately reached out to hug me and softly whispered, "That's what God told me too."

What peace we had. We got up and went out to the dining room and shared our decision.

The weather that day was a mixed bag. It was cloudy, sunny, and every once in a while we felt a few sprinkles. Our children and their cousins waited outside for us. Some were water skiing and wanted to get Bruce out on the pontoon boat so he could go across the lake to watch Blake and Nicole try to get up on skis for the first time. Blake was already in the speedboat and ready to go. They kept calling the cabin with their walkie-talkies to see if we were ready yet. Finally, we called them with our walkie-talkie. We told them about our decision and that Bruce was ready to come out on the boat. Everyone cheered.

Going out on the boat in the hot, humid weather was scary for Bruce. It made breathing difficult, but he trusted God to honor the desires of his heart-to see his children get up on water skis for the first time. The weather was threatening, but once we set out on the pontoon boat, the clouds seemed to clear, and the sun broke through. It felt so good. Bruce sat down for the ride and just beamed.

He was one of the best water skiers I knew. He could slalom like nobody's business, and it meant the world to him to pass this loved tradition on to his children.

Blake was ready. He wanted nothing more than to have his dad witness his first time getting up on water skis. Everyone shouted cheers of encouragement to Blake. It was time. Blake yelled, "Hit it," and Uncle Chuck put the speedboat at full throttle. Right before our eyes, up popped Blake! When I looked over at Bruce, I saw him go from standing and cheering for Blake, to sitting and smiling. Tears began to well up in his eyes. What an honor and privilege God gave him to witness his son get up on skis for the first time. The tears he cried that afternoon were sweet tears of absolute joy. Likewise, Blake experienced the thrill of the cold spray of water on his face and felt the cool breeze singing past his ears. The feeling was freeing and exhilarating. What Bruce and Blake didn't realize was they both had entered the "God Zone" that afternoon.

A "God Zone" is a place we can only get to by totally trusting God. We can't get there on our own accord or by our own power. We need to trust God to carry us through the scariest times of our lives. Until we release all we are and have to Him, totally trust Him, surrender from our comfort zone, we will never experience the ultimate God Zones in our life. It wasn't until Blake got out of the boat, put on the skis and his life jacket, that he felt the pure sense of accomplishment and joy of water skiing for the first time. It wasn't until Bruce got out of the comfort of the cabin and onto the pontoon boat to go across the lake, trusting God to give him strength, that he experienced the ultimate joy of seeing his son water ski for the first time.

What a beautiful ending to a beautiful day.

The Turtle Eggs

The next morning at the cabin, Nicole came quietly into our bedroom. She had been awake for awhile, but Bruce and I had slept in. She whispered I should come quickly. A large turtle had meandered up from the lake and was digging a hole to lay her eggs. She gently grabbed my hand and helped me get out of bed. Everyone else was up and had gathered in another room from which they could see the huge snapping turtle. Its outer shell must have measured two feet in diameter. Sure enough, she was digging a large hole to drop her eggs. Usually she did this every summer down by the lake's shore. By nightfall, the raccoons would find the tasty little morsels and eat a nice little supper. This year the mommy turtle seemed to want to do everything she could to protect these precious little eggs. It was fascinating to watch her. This was nature in her finest. The turtle dug and dug with her strong hind legs. She turned and turned until she had made a complete circle while digging. Then she perched herself on the edge of a rather large hole and waited. I waited with her, coaching her every step of the way.

As I watched her, I had a strong sense from God to "pay attention; this is a sign." I thought it a little strange, but then I had been praying fervently for eyes to see God's hand in all we were going through. I didn't understand what this birthing turtle had to do with anything, but I realized I just needed to watch and learn.

Then it happened: she raised her heavy shell with her strong legs, and out dropped a beautiful white egg. It was about the size of a small chicken egg. I wanted to cheer for her, but I refrained. I didn't want to frighten her birthing session. One by one, beautiful white eggs dropped into the hole. Each time I counted. *One, two, three . . . seven, eight, nine . . . twelve, thirteen, fourteen . . .* Once in a while someone from the family would act as the scout and come into the bedroom to ask what number the mommy turtle was now on. The entire process lasted about two hours. I was diligent, never taking my eyes off the turtle. *Twenty, twenty-one, twenty-two . . . thirty, thirty-one, thirty-two.*

Bruce had gotten up by now and peered over my shoulder to watch the show. Putting his hand on my shoulder, he asked,

"How long are you going to watch her, and why are you counting all the eggs?"

"Until she's finished," I replied. "And you remember how I've been praying for eyes to see God's presence? Well, for some strange reason I'm sure this is some sign from God. I'm not sure what it means, but someday I'll know. I just need to watch."

Thirty-six, thirty-seven, thirty-eight. Shoot. Was that an egg? Her thick leg was in the way. I couldn't see if an egg fell. She raised her tired body just like all the other times when she dropped an egg, but this time she turned a little, and I couldn't see the egg. Was that thirty-nine? She rested a few minutes, and then with all the strength she could muster, her tired body shook as she raised her shell one last time. *Forty—or was it thirty nine?*

She was finished. No more eggs dropped, and she began the process of covering them. After she finished, she slowly ambled down to the lake. When she made it to the water's edge, she disappeared into the refreshing lake, never to return to her deposit of eggs. Everyone wanted to know how many she dropped, because they had a bet going. I felt so bad because I wasn't sure if it was 39 or 40. But maybe I wasn't supposed to know.

All day long I couldn't get those turtle eggs out of my head. *I knew they meant something, but what?* Suddenly it came to me. *Bruce was 39-years-old, and in a few weeks he would celebrate his 40th birthday. It had something to do with Bruce, but what?* We talked about the eggs and the unusual experience that morning. Mal, my father-in-law, said that if the raccoons got a whiff of the eggs they'd be history. The very thought of that horrified me. We can't let those babies get eaten! The raccoons have eaten the eggs every year. Not this year! The mommy turtle went to all that trouble to birth them on high ground, where it was safer.

After much family discussion over brunch, and my insistence that we needed to do all we could do to save the turtle eggs, we made a plan. Mal, my father-in-law, and John, my brother-in-law, went into town with their supply list. They came back and began "Operation Save the Baby Turtles." They dug a trench around the perimeter of the birthing bed and constructed a tall fence that would be secured in place. Nothing would get in to disturb or interfere with the development of those forming turtles. We cooperatively did all we could to save the eggs. Now it was out of our hands and in God's.

When we returned home from the cabin I hopped on the Internet and researched information about the snapping turtle. I discovered the gestation period is approximately one hundred days. That meant the turtles should be hatching sometime the end of September. We planned to open the fence around that time so they would be able to freely leave and get to the lake.

All summer long we'd walk by and talk to the turtles buried under ground. All summer long we made sure the fencing was secure and did whatever we could to protect the fragile, help-less eggs. Every member of our family seemed to have some part in "Operation Save the Baby Turtles." Summer came and went, and then fall started nipping at our heels. By the end of September there were no baby turtles. Then came October and still no baby turtles.

In late September Mal and I got a shovel and unearthed an egg. Yep, they were still there, but no turtles had formed in the egg we checked. We decided to leave the rest alone and give them more time.

John and Kyle were up to the cabin in October and decided to check out the eggs again. They found the eggs, but for whatever reason, they never hatched. Not one. The baby turtles couldn't be saved no matter how hard we all tried to save them.

Then I got scared.

I was reminded of the day I watched the mommy turtle birth those eggs, and somehow I knew it was a sign from God. I knew it had to do with Bruce. Specifically, I knew it had to do with Bruce being 39 going on 40. At the time the turtle dropped the eggs, Bruce was 39. Now he was 40. There was a direct correlation. Was the fact that the baby turtles died in spite of every possible thing that we did for them a premonition of things to come with Bruce? Would he not see his 41st birthday despite everything the doctors and those who loved him did for him? I couldn't bear to think about it. Yet somehow I knew it to be true. God was preparing me.

Chapter 10

A Job Moment

The Circle of Life

Unable to get the turtle eggs out of my mind, I reflected on life and mortality. I contemplated its beginning and end and how it ultimately affects each of us. Knowing that life has a cycle, and we are each somewhere in the middle, I came to a realization about my own frailties.

I thought about how a typical life cycle might look. We're born, and then we grow from newborns to infants to toddlers. The entire time we need people to care for our every need, because without people, we wouldn't survive. We begin to learn the basic necessities of life such as how to feed and dress ourselves. Boo boo's are usually kissed away by our mommy or daddy, and we continue to need their loving arms wrapped around us when the world becomes too big and scary. Preschool arrives and we're gradually learning to become independent.

Before we realize it we've entered elementary school and are totally self-sufficient. At least in all areas except transportation, paying for the food we eat, providing shelter and other amenities. By the end of fifth grade, we can surf the net, e-mail and instant message friends, chat on Mom's cell phone, and do all the three R's—reading, writing, and arithmetic. We even know the latest fashion and who's who in the music industry. And our parents are only cool when we say they are cool.

Elementary school comes and goes, and then there's junior high. Now that we've mastered everything there is to master in life . . . hormones come into the picture. We have no idea what's up or down, and our parents don't know if they should smack us a good one up along side our head or kiss away our boo-boo's like they used to. Frankly, we have no clue either, so parents and children live in a turbulent world.

Eighth grade graduation arrives, and high school awaits us. We're at the stage in life where everything evolves all around *me*. When can I drive a car? Better yet, when do I get my own car? What about dating? Curfews? Who needs them? I no longer need my mom, and heaven forbid if my parents give me a hug in public. Who needs family gatherings; I'd rather be with my friends, thank you very much! And so it goes.

Then there's high school graduation, and all that was familiar and comfortable becomes scary and unfamiliar. A higher education usually awaits us, and now we are completely on our own. We've pushed to be independent since we learned to walk, and now we're walking right out of the place we call home. The place that taught us every thing we now know. It's scary and confusing, yet we know we must walk alone. Mom or Dad can no longer hold our hands, and they will no longer be there to catch us when we fall. We've asked for this independence all along, and now it's ours.

Suddenly our appreciation for our parents makes a drastic shift. They did know something after all! Even though these thoughts of appreciation for our parents creep into our thoughts, we stuff them down deep because we're on our own now! Who needs anyone? Besides, there's a whole new world out there to discover and conquer. Maturity sets in, we earn a college diploma, and the real world awaits us. We land a job, accumulate college debt up to our eyeballs, and the bills don't stop coming in the mail. Now, throw in a marriage, a baby or two, a job promotion, a house, and the stresses of life are weighing heavily upon our shoulders.

Help!

What happened to the good 'ol days? What happened to boo-boo's being erased by our mommy's kisses? Suddenly we slap ourselves in the face while looking in the mirror. We're the parents now. "Rise to the occasion," we tell ourselves. We raise our children as our parents raised us, only we stubbornly use new techniques. Times are different, we tell ourselves. Before we know it, we are empty nesters. Our own parents are aging and have health problems. Now we need to care for the very people who used to care for us! What's up with that? At some point we sit down with a cup of coffee, stare out in space, and think, "Is this all there is?"

For the first time we think about mortality, and we get scared. No one raised us and talked about death. No one told us we wouldn't live forever. We were young, invincible, and thought we were out to conquer the world. We begin to realize that the big "S" on our chest no longer stands for Superman or Superwoman, but rather "surrender." A paralyzing feeling blankets us. We no longer have control. We are much smaller than we ever imagined, and we feel alone. We're older and would like to think we're wiser. We now understand what "letting go and letting God" means. A crossroad in life stands before us, and the very one who created us stands at the "Y." He's holding out His hand. Will we grab the Father's hand humbly in surrender or tough it alone under the guise of a superhero?

Oh, the circle of life . . .

My wandering thoughts returned to the present.

The Request

Just as our family tried to save the turtle eggs, so many people rallied around Bruce. He was surrounded with the best medical care, support from work, and many family and friends who loved him so much. We never ceased being amazed at God's unending love for us through the acts of kindness of others.

Toward the end of May, our pastor and Bruce's friend Paul Froland asked him about hosting a benefit for our family. Many were concerned about the medical costs that we would incur and wanted to do something to help. Friends from Good Shepherd Community, Bruce's previous employer, and Trinity Lutheran Church, where we were members, had already discussed this and agreed to co-sponsor the event. Bruce's initial reaction was to say no to the benefit. He told them to use the money for someone who could really use it. He didn't want to put anyone out. Benefits happened to other people. I don't think he had a full grasp of what was happening to him. It was still so surreal.

Bruce was a sick man, and this type of illness was nothing anyone could fix. Medical bills started pouring in, and even though he had insurance through his employer, we still had a mound of bills to pay. We had just begun the discussions about going to the second cancer facility and knew that the HMO we were under wouldn't support payment to an out-of-network medical facility. My administrator job would end soon, and Bruce was unable to work anymore. He had eight weeks of sick time saved up, which is so ironic because he had been so healthy up to this time. Now that sick time would come in handy, but it would be gone before we knew it.

After giving much thought to the benefit idea, Bruce told Pastor Paul he would agree to it if there was a prayer and healing service instead. It was just like him to think of the spiritual needs instead of the physical and temporal needs. He also requested that the service be for everyone who had physical needs, not just him. I'm sure Pastor Paul just shook his head at Bruce's request. It was so typical. We reached a compromise. Bruce would get his service. Anyone who attended and wanted to come forward for a prayer and blessings could do so. But a benefit would still be held to assist with his medical expenses. A few dates were suggested.

"The sooner, the better," Bruce's friend Paul said.

There was a sense of urgency among the groups that were planning the event. Paul mentioned the dates, and one stuck out at me: June 26. That was it—perfect! June 26th was Bruce's 40th birthday. Instead of gathering together for a gloomy event, it could be a celebration of his life.

I spoke with Bruce about the date and he agreed. He liked the idea of a celebration instead of gathering together under the ominous clouds that hung over him. This was a very difficult time for us, yet God was teaching us another valuable lesson about accepting help.

One day, I was leaving school when Pastor Paul arrived. He walked toward my van and inquired about how Bruce was doing. I told him Bruce was experiencing some of his roughest days. Then I asked about the plans for the benefit. "Has anyone thought of contacting St. Cloud State University? What about Chamber of Commerce friends or the . . .?"

Pastor Paul stopped me mid sentence. "Don't worry about it. The committee has already thought about it, and everything is being taken care of. You need to concentrate on taking care of Bruce and let others plan the event. There are very capable people working out all the details."

"But, it's so hard to accept help. We feel so undeserving . . ."

Then Pastor Paul told me something I will always remember.

"You need to let go of worrying about the benefit and simply let others help. Everyone really feels bad, and we all feel so helpless when it comes to Bruce. People can't just sit around and do nothing; they not only want to help, they need to help." Then he firmly said, "We need to do this for us!"

I had never looked at it that way before. That's love! I didn't ask questions after that.

Bruce had one last request for Pastor Paul: "Can I give the message at the prayer and healing service?"

Bruce has always been a man of many words, and watch out if you stick a microphone in front of him. Pastor Paul agreed, but was concerned if Bruce was physically up to the challenge.

Bruce replied, "If God wants me to speak, he'll provide a way."

Pastor Paul planned a back up message just in case. Now it was up to God. We prayed fervently that Bruce would have the strength to speak. The week before the service, he found a pocket of good time, sat with his laptop, and typed out what he wanted to say. So far, God was coming through for him, but the real test was about to come.

The Benefit

The day had finally come. Bruce was able to speak at his prayer and healing service. Praise Almighty God! The weather was absolutely beautiful—in the low 80s, with a slight breeze. It was also Bruce's 40th birthday. A momentous birthday in human eyes, but in God's eyes, every birthday is as precious as the last. Bruce wore new, tan Dockers that fit him better than all of his other pants. He had on a beautiful green polo shirt, brown belt, and wore his comfortable tennis shoes. Despite his condition, he beamed a heavenly glow that day.

We arrived on time and were greeted by a myriad of people. Cars were everywhere, and without our handicapped parking sticker we would have had to walk for blocks. As we got out of the car, the aroma of barbecue filled the air and welcomed us. Many people stood outside behind large commercial grills with spatulas and tongs in hand. Sporting white aprons, they flipped burgers and brats; all the while, constant chatter and laughter filled the air. It was music to our ears as we entered the foyer of the school that led to the gym.

Immediately, many people greeted us; they seemed to come from everywhere. Even residents from the nursing home worked the tables. They all loved Bruce. Everyone was working together to do this for us. Baskets were filled with colored hearts. People were asked to write memories of Bruce. The hearts would later be assembled into a precious memory book for Blake and Nicole. There were decorations everywhere. A greeter made sure that all who entered signed the guest book. At the end of the day, more than 600 people had signed the guest book. We were told that an additional 100 went directly to the prayer and healing service and never signed the book.

Ladies from our church sat at one of the front tables selling our church cookbook. The proceeds went to Bruce. How wonderful! There was a basket for "benefit" cards, and another basket was just for "birthday" cards and gifts.

We could barely get into the gym. Long tables filled the gym floor. Hundreds of people were already seated and eating. Servers were dishing up plates of food, and Boy Scouts were in full uniform clearing tables and serving beverages. The walls were filled with "Get Well" banners that the school children had made. We were completely overwhelmed, and it was difficult to fight back tears of gratitude. I finally was able to sit down, but I never did eat; I was concerned about Bruce and made sure he ate something. He was his usual social self and just beamed from head to toe. These people were there for him—how awesome was that! How humbling.

Tables dotted the lawn too. At some point, one of my girlfriends took my hand and led me outside to show me there were just as many people outside as there were inside. It was a beautiful sight. Co-workers came from Bruce's previous jobs, members of our church, parents, teachers, board members, and kids from the school. We saw community leaders, family, neighbors, and people from our hometowns, college friends, friends from when Bruce studied in England, and many more. It was totally overwhelming, yet so uplifting.

When it was time for the prayer and healing service, we walked over to the church. By now, the church was packed to the rafters with people. Overflow went to the church basement, where the service was being broadcast on a big screen. The service was videotaped and would become a mighty and powerful witnessing tool in the months to come. Praise music filled the church sanctuary as we entered. Beautiful music flooded the church like nothing I've ever heard before, and I'm sure it could be heard from blocks away. The Spirit was present in our church, and I felt like the ceiling on our church building lifted from its studs and hovered over all of us most of the service.

Music was always so special and personal to us. The Sunday after Bruce found out he had cancer, we sang with the worship leaders' team. It was always such a focus of our ministry at church.

After all the beautiful music and many angelic solos, it was time for Bruce to speak. Pastor Paul even teased Bruce about how dangerous it was to put a microphone in front of him, but then he trusted that he would take this opportunity for God's glory. A well-padded and plush swivel barstool with a supportive back was placed at the front of the sanctuary. The expensive chair was a loner from a local furniture store. A small stand was set next to the swivel chair with a glass of water on it. A single microphone stood in front of it. They had thought of everything! Pastor Paul gave a brief introduction before Bruce spoke. Despite how he felt, God in His grace and mercy held Bruce that evening in the very palm of His hand and gave him the strength to share the message He had laid upon Bruce's heart just weeks earlier.

The "Job Moment"

Earlier I'd said that I would explain Bruce's "Job Moment." It's time. However, no one can explain it better than Bruce himself, so I'm not going to attempt to upstage him. He related his "Job Moment" in the message he gave at the prayer and healing service. Bruce began:

"This could be difficult for me tonight. You know I'm a man of few words, quiet, shy, and introverted. As unaccustomed as I am to public speaking, I may struggle somewhat, and I pray you'll bear with me for the next couple of hours." Laughter erupted.

"Oh, did I mention I have cancer? Oh yeah, you folks probably know that by now. On behalf of my precious soul mate and wife, Lynn, the second best undeserved gift I've received from God (I'll tell you about the first in a minute), and on behalf of my son, Blake, and daughter, Nicole, we want to thank each and every one of you for coming tonight. It is indeed humbling and overwhelming. We especially want you to join us in thanking all the people who made this event happen, out of their love and concern for us, and in service to Almighty God." Bruce led the gathering in a much-deserved applause.

"I know that most, if not all of you, believe that you are here tonight for me and my family. But as I've prayed about this event, I am convinced that many of you are here tonight because God wanted you to be here—for you.

"On Thursday, April 25th, I was on lunchtime at home. I received the call with my test results. A CT scan showed tumors that were presenting themselves in multiple places. In one phone call, our lives were completely and traumatically changed. Later, a liver biopsy confirmed what we already knew in our hearts—stage IV Adenocarcinoma of lung primary. I've never smoked, and I don't drink. I try to stay in shape and eat a 'B' diet.

"I experienced increasing pain, and so I've started taking narcotic painkillers that seem to bring about nausea and constipation. The Mayo Clinic has confirmed the diagnosis and treatment plan. A MRI scan showed that one of my cancerous vertebrae was closing around my spinal cord, and we began radiation there and to my head, where tumors had started. On May 10, our 16th wedding anniversary, I began chemotherapy.

"I've finished two cycles of chemotherapy, and just yesterday, got results of my second CT scan, which shows that the cancer has not responded thus far and is in fact worse. So, in God's mysterious plan, this prayer and healing service comes at the perfect time.

"It would be insensitive of me to catalog the ways in which I suffered thus far, because I know there are those here who have suffered far worse, so I won't do that. What I do want to share is how what I've gone through so far has brought a whole new perspective on the most significant moment in all of our lives.

"Who is Jesus Christ? You know—Son of God, Lord of Lords, and Savior of the world. But who is He *really*? To me, He's the part of God that is seeable and knowable. So our best description is Son of God. But Jesus was a real man. No halo, no permanently white, unsoiled robe. He sweat, ate, got dirty and smelly, went to the bathroom, and squinted into bright sun.

"In short, God walked among us. Why? Because we had messed up, broken His laws for us (better known as the Ten Commandments), and we were toast because nobody was, or is, able to keep these laws. Because we all have an inherited form of cancer—it's called a sinful nature. We are inclined to hurt, cheat, steal, lie, disobey, even when we try our best not to.

"Jesus preached about what God really desired for us—to be reunited with Him. Better said, *reconciled* to Him and *forgiven*, in a bond that would never break and would lead us to love and serve people with abundant joy. He came to tell of the great news. The great news, though, was a totally irrational event! His three-year ministry consisted of telling of the coming kingdom of God, of casting out demons, and of healing people; He even brought several people back to life who had been dead. This stuff really happened. The Bible is the most corroborated collection of writings from the ancient world.

"After all these incredible events comes this irrational event. I mean, here's Jesus—a real man, but also really God— literally unable to sin. He didn't break even one of the Ten Commandments. Then, what did we do? We killed Him, even though He had done nothing wrong.

"Why? That's the irrational plan. How? In the most horrible way possible. He suffered grievously in the body and the mind, even though He knew it could be stopped in an instant. Romans 8:17 (NLT) reads, 'And since we are his children, we will share his treasures—for everything God gives to his Son, Christ, is ours, too. But if we are to share his glory, we must also share his suffering.'

"Share in His suffering? That's my journey. Christ's sufferings have never been so real or understandable to me then they are right now. He knew what He would face. He told His disciples. And yet, He faced betrayal, He was flogged with a lead-tipped whip, producing horrific open wounds across his back. He was beaten with a stick on his head. If that wasn't enough, they jammed a crown of thorns on His head, mocked Him, and spit on Him.

"Then, there was His grief and spiritual agony. Matthew 26:38 reads, 'He told them, "My soul is crushed with grief to the point of death. Stay here and watch with me."' He prayed more fervently, and He was in such agony of spirit that His sweat fell to the ground like great drops of blood, which is found in Luke 22:44.

"That's exactly how I felt finding out I had cancer.

"Then, came the crucifixion. Described by a medical doctor who researched the physical dynamics of this capital punishment and concluded that it is the most painful method of death man ever invented.

"Picture this—spikes going through his wrists and feet." Bruce pointed to each of his own wrists. Then holding both of his arms stretching out and up, he continued. "The death actually came by asphyxiation, with the only way to get a breath was to push up against the spikes to make a breath even possible." After demonstrating in his weakened state, Bruce gradually relaxed his arms, slowly lowering them to his side.

"Finally, the reality hits me. Dying like this was to pay for the sins of Bruce MacKenzie and every other person. It would mean real separation from God for the first time. Mark 15:34 says, 'Then, at that time Jesus called out with a loud voice, "*Eloi, Eloi, lema sabachthani?*" which means, "My God, my God, why have you forsaken me?"' Jesus Christ went to hell, separated from God, because that's the price of my sins, your sins, and every one who ever will live or has lived sins.

"But the rest of the story is the key. He rose again from the dead. He conquered death as only God could do and was later seen by hundreds of his followers before He returned to be with God the Father. You see, He suffered and died in Bruce MacKenzie's place to pay for Bruce MacKenzie's sin. That is the greatest undeserved gift I've received from God. It's your undeserved gift too. There's nothing you have to do to get right with God here. Unlike Islam, Buddhism, Hinduism, New Age religious approaches, which outline what we must do to reach nirvana, this Christian faith is a done deal. It was done over 2000 years ago. It's simply a gift that I stop refusing to accept.

"My prayer for those of you who are here tonight is that this message would pierce your heart. That it has hit a cord. You know that something has been missing in your life—you don't have a deep peace and sense of purpose and meaning in your life—a sense that your past mistakes will keep you from getting to heaven.

"My prayer is that you accept this free gift of Jesus Christ and the forgiveness and new life that it brings. Do it tonight. I promise you, you'll never regret it. Not even if you get advanced cancer.

"On one particularly difficult day some weeks ago, I read in 1 Peter 4:12, 13, which says, 'Dear friends, do not be surprised at the painful trial that you are now suffering, as though something strange were happening to you. But rejoice that you participate in the sufferings of Christ, so that you may be overjoyed when his glory is revealed.' That verse made me look back in the Bible at Job. You remember him? I'll paraphrase a bit.

"Job was a righteous man before God. He was keeping the law, so Satan goes to God and talks about Job, and he says that Job won't follow God anymore if he really gets hit hard. So God allows Satan to take a whack, but not to kill him. In one evening, really in about fifteen minutes, Job finds out that all his extensive flocks of oxen, donkeys, sheep, and camels have been slaughtered or stolen, and all ten of his children were killed when their house collapsed. That's like losing all your children, your house, your cars, your bank accounts, and your 401K all in one evening.

"What was Job's response? 'Why me God?' 'Oh God, what have I done wrong to deserve this?' or 'God, I don't deserve this; look at all I've done for you. I hate you for this!' No. Job's response is found in Job 1:20, 'At this, Job got up and tore his robe and shaved his head.'" Bruce paused for a moment, running his hand across the top of his balding head, smiled, then continued. People erupted in laughter.

"'Then he fell to the ground in worship and said: "Naked I came from my mother's womb, and naked will I depart. The Lord gave and the Lord has taken away, may the name of the

Lord be praised." In all of this, Job did not sin by charging God with wrongdoing.' He worshipped God at this radical, life-changing avalanche of tragedy. What would your response have been?

"My 'Job Moment' came when I hung up the phone on April 25. I fell to my knees against the chair and cried out to God in a loud voice. It came from my soul, I didn't think about what to say, because my mind was swirling. I said: 'God, this has got to be all about You, it's got to be You; it's got to be You in me, because I have nothing inside me to deal with this. I don't know where to begin. God, please hold me and carry me.'

"He has never stopped answering that prayer, and He never will. And this, my friends in Christ, is why many of you have remarked at how well I've taken this and the peace that we have (as a family). How I have this passion to share Christ and share these incredible insights and blessings—yes, blessings. There are abundant blessings that this cancer and all that it means have brought us. It has nothing to do with me. It has everything to do with who God is, what He promises us, and whether we trust Him enough to walk with Him wherever we must go.

"I do.

"Suffering produces a unique opportunity for the Christian. It's either curse God or thank Him, praise Him, and follow Him. This is another incredibly irrational opportunity for us as Christians.

"And so it comes down to this. Do we really trust Him, or don't we? Are we patty-caking our Christianity when it suits us, or are we ready to be disciples who will follow Christ wherever He leads us? The blessings are often hidden and incredible.

"Later on, I read 1 Peter 4:1–2, 'Therefore, since Christ suffered in his body, arm yourselves also with the same attitude, because he who has suffered in his body is done with sin. As a result, he does not live the rest of his earthly life for evil human desires, but for the will of God.' The word picture I got was of the washtub ringer. If you recall, the shirt is fed through the rollers, and it gets squeezed to within an inch of its life. While it's being pulled through, the water is pushed out. Just like that sinful desire, as you surrender to what God's plan is, you are pulled through it and receive a very special blessing and a burning desire to serve Him.

"Now, before you start marveling at me, let me tell you this suffering sucks. For me and for those who love me. It's still no fun. I still think of how I used to feel and wonder if I will ever feel great again. I doubt. I get scared. But I tell these things to God and He listens. And He understands because His own Son, Jesus, told him the very same things.

"To illustrate this, we'd like to share a poem that my wife, Lynn, wrote during a period of great agony she felt over a woman she was ministering to in her Bible Study Fellowship class who was suffering miserably with cancer. In Lynn's time of agony, prayer, and tears, this poem rushed through her mind and spilled onto paper. She has never altered a word from the original draft, and she knows that these words were God's answer to that prayer of agony. My sister, Kyle, has agreed to read it."

The Tear Catcher

Suffering beyond all understanding
Suffering more than one can bear . . .

"When did I say that I wouldn't stay?
When did I say it wouldn't hurt?

Hear me, for my words are clear.

Nothing!
I say, nothing is too great
that the two of us can't bear!

Together,
not alone
—That was never in the plan.

Don't you know that when you invited me into your heart,
I would not only stay forever,
But I would become your main artery
—your only life line.

Oh, how you take me for granted.
Don't you know, I've been here all along.
Feel my touch
Feel my warmth
Feel your weight
become light as I hold you.

Let go of your apprehensions
Let go of your fears
Lay your head on my shoulder
and
I'll catch your tears."

"Your Job Moment will come. You'll know it, if it already hasn't. Some thing will come in your life—a death, health condition, job loss, marriage crisis, betrayal of friendship, something. God will be waiting to be asked to hold, guide, and lead you through it so that a greater plan of His can unfold for you.

"The question will be, 'Do I trust Him? Really trust Him? Trust Him enough to follow Him and surrender to Him even into this dark, hideous forest of suffering?' I promise you'll never regret it, and you'll be blown away by the blessings that will come. You know folks, this is the only day we know we've got for sure. We walk in God's grace every day. We have no idea what tomorrow will bring. It might be more of the same old, same old, or it might be your Job Moment.

"I beg each of you to treasure each day He gives you. Accept Christ today. Treat those you love as though what you say today will be their last memory of you. Ask to be forgiven now. Kiss your wife hello and goodbye, passionately. Turn off the television and play with your kids. Call your dear friend. Share the gospel of Christ with someone close to you who doesn't know Him. Do it today. Do it now. Resolve right now to walk out of here a changed person, a new follower of Jesus Christ. A person filled with passion to serve others. Give your smoking habit to God and trust, and He'll remove the desire. Eat lots of fruits and vegetables to prevent cancer. Whatever it is, resolve it, give it to God, pray about it, trust Him and let Him change you forever.

"Thanks for listening and may God bless each of you."

• Chapter 11 •

By Being Formed, We Become Transformed

The "Ah-Ha" Moments in Life

The prayer and healing service was a memorable moment in time during our cancer journey, and it caused me to reflect back on my life and generations of lives before me. It reminded me of those times when life actually made sense for a moment. I like to call them the "Ah-ha" moments in life.

How many times had I looked back over a period in my life and said, "Ah, now I get it"? Or, it felt like someone took the palm of his or her hand and slapped it on my forehead in an "Ah-ha" moment? Regardless of how or when it came, at some point the messiness of my life took shape, and things began to make sense. Sometimes, it looked like what I expected it would all along, and other times it took on a shape that I never expected; but, nevertheless, the shape started to form something.

I'm reminded of a time I was at our church's adult Sunday morning Bible study. My son, who had just been let out of Sunday School early, came over to me and handed me a hard lump of cold, gray clay. The assignment was to form a boat out of it. I believe his class was learning about when Peter got out of the boat to walk on water. Blake handed me this lump of clay and asked me to hold it for him. He said he was frustrated, because the clay was supposed to be molded into a boat and it wouldn't cooperate. As quickly as he appeared, he disappeared.

I didn't think twice about the hard lump of clay that rested in the palm of my hand. Blake was gone, and my attention went back to the Bible study topic at hand. As time went by, my warm hands cradled the clay as if to nurture it back to health. It became warm. Without realizing it, my fingers wrapped around the hard, gray mound of clay and seemed to be transforming it. What was once cold and hard slowly became soft and pliable. Gently, I started to form the hard lump of clay into the boat it was intended to be from the beginning. It was easy and seemed natural.

Then, I had one of those "Ah-ha" moments. I realized that we are like lumps of clay—hard and stiff. It isn't until God sets His right hand under us that we start to soften up. Before we know it, we are soft and pliable and are able to be formed into the very being that God intended for us all along. The key is we need to allow ourselves to completely surrender. God will then form and transform us.

As for Bruce and me, our lives were like clay; we were being formed and changed every day. It happened right before our very eyes. So much had happened, yet the greater purpose that God had in store for us seemed to be hanging in the loom. I didn't understand the reason for this affliction, yet I felt God was leading us down this road for a greater purpose. It was a road I never thought we'd travel. I needed to blindly trust, because I couldn't see beyond the haze that surrounded me.

By now, Bruce had gone through all the "firsts" that cancer could introduce. It came in a variety of ways—as a new type of fear, relentless chemo, anger, radiation, doubt, unfamiliar pains, questions, new drugs, nausea . . . and the list continued. As time went by, I found the e-mails became more specific, more detailed, and because of this they were naturally forming a story. That story was not only telling our story, but also it ultimately told God's story. No longer were we just asking for specific prayer and telling the details of our journey; but rather, we were telling of the "God sightings" we were privileged to witness along the way. We saw sides of God that we would have never encountered if we had not allowed His mighty hands to form us and carry us down this rugged path.

The New Treatment Plan

We were excited to be at the new cancer treatment center. Our oncologist took time to answer all our questions and really showed that she cared for the person but hated the cancer. We were ready to fight a new battle, and there was a team of medical experts to assist in the war. Up to this point, we were praying that Bruce's medical insurance would pay for the new cancer treatment, because the plan we had said absolutely "No" to out-of-network referrals. Through a letter from Bruce and many phone calls, the insurance company not only agreed to cover the out-of-network consult, but also agreed to pay for a portion of the treatment. We were so thankful. This was huge. After a consult, exam, and several tests, they were able to formulate a new treatment plan. He now had a stress fracture in his lower lumbar due to the cancer in the bones. For the moment, they would just keep a close eye on it.

Immediately, Bruce received new mixes of chemo drugs. Two months went by, and finally, new tests were taken. The cancer in the brain showed no visible lesions, and the "peppered" effect that was in the liver was less in number and size. I continued updating the Prayer Warriors, and he continued being a great patient. At one point I thought he was simply delirious, because he started quoting Scripture, only he adjusted it slightly.

He said, "Yea, though I walk through the valley of the shadow of chemo . . ."

I laughed when he said that. I think he coined a new phrase; even his doctors laughed when we told them.

In person and through e-mails, people asked how our children were doing. My answer usually was "remarkably well." They hurt for their dad and wished that life as they knew it could return to normal. We traveled this road together and prayed constantly with them for specific needs. We were trying to teach them "how" to travel through these tough times. We didn't have all the answers, and that's why we had to rely on God's word and trust in His promises. We learned that children are never too young to learn God's wonderful promises and truths. Many times, they are far more accepting of them than adults. In the meantime, we asked God to teach us whatever we needed to learn from Him during these times, and we clung to Scripture and His promises to us.

I especially love 2 Corinthians 8:10. This is when Paul, being tempted by Satan, said, "Three times I pleaded with the Lord to take it away from me. But he said to me, 'My grace is sufficient for you, for my power is made perfect in weakness.' Therefore I will boast all the more gladly about my weaknesses, so that Christ's power may rest on me. That is why, for Christ's sake, I delight in weakness, in insults, in hardships, in persecutions, in difficulties. For when I am weak, then I am strong." I saw this verse as just another one of God's great dichotomies—when I am weak, then I am strong . . . the first shall be last and the last shall be first . . . it is by grace alone that you are saved, not by works lest any man should boast . . . and the list goes on.

Who would ever imagine that their healthy, active 40-year-old husband would get such a horrible disease? Not me. But then I'm learning not to question or blame God; instead I ask Him to show and teach me how to deal with tough situations in a way that would make Him proud. I don't always do a good job of that, and the road is rather bumpy at times, but I always know He's there right beside me, taking the pebbles out of my shoes.

The Conferences

The Promise Keepers conference was scheduled for the weekend after Labor Day. Bruce looked forward to attending. Promise Keepers is a Christ-centered organization which introduces men to Jesus Christ as their Savior and Lord and then helps them grow as Christians.

Days before the conference, Bruce went to Parker Hughes Cancer Center for blood work and a check up. His platelet count had plummeted. It was at 20,000 and should have been over 140,000. They wouldn't even let us leave the Twin Cities until Bruce received a transfusion of platelets. This was his first transfusion. The next day, he had another blood test taken to see if the transfusion helped. His bags were packed as he waited for the call from his doctor to give him the "all clear" to attend Promise Keepers. Just minutes before they were scheduled to leave, he got the call and was cleared to go.

God's grace and presence were evident at Promise Keepers. At one point the men stood in lines outside to pick up their box lunches. The process took over 45 minutes. With more than 11,000 hungry men to contend with, Bruce was just a speck in the sea of testosterone. Most guys didn't mind the wait, but for Bruce it was a challenge. That particular weekend the weather was very hot and humid. Because of the cancer in his lungs and collapsed right lung, hot and humid weather was devastating to his breathing. He told me that just when he was beginning to feel overcome by the heat and humidity, God blew a breath of cool air on him that sustained him beyond his wildest imagination. That was only one example of God's provisions for him, but one I feel is important to share. It's the little things for which we don't give God credit. And in Bruce's case, breathing was especially important! He came home overjoyed, thankful, and tired.

The next weekend, I was able to attend the Women of Faith conference at the Xcel Energy Center in St. Paul. Women of Faith is similar to Promise Keepers, only it's for women. What a blessing it was to get away and enjoy some "girlfriend" time. Once again, God took good care of Bruce while I was gone. I returned on September 14th, which was our son's 13th birthday. A teenager—what an interesting age!

At the Women of Faith conference, one of the speakers seemed to speak directly to me (actually they all did), but the following Scripture surpassed them all: "Do not be anxious about anything, but in everything, by prayer and petition, with thanksgiving, present your requests to God. And the peace of God, which transcends all understanding, will guard your hearts and your minds in Christ Jesus." That is from Philippians 4:6–7. The speaker personalized it for herself, and I've since personalized it for me. Here goes:

> Do not be anxious *(which this "cancer thing" has tended to make me!)* about anything *(which means the same as no-thing)*, but in everything *(I guess that includes this cancer invasion, right God?)*, by prayer *(we're all doing that)* and petition *(I'm pleading my heart out, Lord)*, with thanksgiving *(now wait just one bloody minute, Lord! Thanksgiving? With Bruce having terminal cancer, you expect me to be thankful? I think not. Okay, okay, I'll read on)*, present your requests to God. *(Lord I'm crying out, are you hearing me?)* And the peace of God *(boy, I could sure use some of "God's peace")*, which transcends all understanding *(that's the real cool thing, Lord;*

*I've felt that peace, and it doesn't make any sense
to me. It's a peace I don't understand . . . it's "light
years" beyond my understanding),* will guard your
hearts *(mine's pretty fragile right now)* and your
minds *(my mind can hardly digest what seems to
be the "new normal in our lives")* in Christ Jesus.
*(Thank you God for all your many provisions—
through Christ Jesus.)*

Wow! What a way to read Scripture.

The Pump Organ

It was the middle of October, and summer struggled to
hang on. Bruce and I were traveling to a healing crusade in
Des Moines, Iowa. From central Minnesota, we calculated we'd
have approximately a six-hour drive.

It had only been a little over five months since the diagnosis.
Bruce said he was up for the trip. Mom agreed to watch the
kids. My brother and wife lived in Des Moines, so we could stay
with them. We decided we'd travel the distance and see where
God would lead us. It wasn't so much the crusade that made
an impact on us that particularly beautiful October weekend;
but rather, it was an event that happened along the way. Out
of nowhere, a wonderful thing took place that had nothing to
do with anything (but then that's just like God to deal with the
nothingness in our lives!).

Since the diagnosis of Bruce's cancer, I had done most of
the driving. We had already been on the road more than three
hours when we stopped for lunch. It wasn't long, and we were
back on the road again. Bruce saw I was getting sleepy, so he
volunteered to drive. After twenty minutes of watching him
slap his face, I was once again behind the wheel. Still tired, I

too started slapping my face. I decided to pull over at the first stop we could.

"Look," Bruce said, "there's a 'Welcome Center' coming up."

I took the next exit. In a short time, I realized that to get to the Welcome Center I needed to head south two miles. *Strange*, I thought, but I continued on. Bruce thought I was crazy to go off the interstate that far just to wake up, but he wasn't driving. The signs leading to the Welcome Center were one right after another. They were intriguing, and there was no way I was going to turn around now. First, there was a sign that read: "Welcome Center-2 miles," then "Walldrug-453 miles," then: "almost there," "not quite," "getting closer," "a little further" . . . and the signs continued. By this time, I was really curious. Nothing would stop me now.

The two miles seemed like an eternity. We finally arrived in a quaint, tiny town called Dows, Iowa. A huge grain elevator greeted us on the left, and a set of train tracks and a parked train greeted us on the right. I felt like I was swept away to another place, another era. We finally arrived at the Welcome Center, and I stopped the car. It was actually an old train depot that had been reconstructed into a Welcome Center/museum.

By this time, my eyelids were heavy, so I decided to get out of the car and walk. I walked on a dirt road that ran parallel to the city park. The park consisted of two park benches and one picnic table. It was next to several turn-of-the-century houses and an old brick church. A car drove past, and an elderly gentleman waved to me. Out of courtesy, I waved back sheepishly. The afternoon was beautiful. The air was crisp, a balmy 65 degrees. Birds were chirping, the sun was shining, and a crisp, refreshing smell was in the air. I was starting to wake up and enjoy God's creation.

As I walked back to the car, I noticed the Welcome Center. *I've driven this far off the beaten track,* I thought to myself, *I*

might as well see what it was that brought me to this quaint town.
I walked up the ramp and entered; Bruce was still kicked back
in the Caravan seat to catch a few *ZZZ's*. As I walked into
this tiny building from the past, I suddenly felt taken back in
time—like I was being swept away to the 1800–1900s. Upon
entering, I was greeted by a little, old man, who was not much
taller than I. He had stark white, thick hair and a mustache.
There was a distinctive twinkle in his eyes. He appeared to be
in his 80s, and if I looked closely enough, it seemed as if he
had simply jumped off the yellowed pages of history right into
that museum.

Before I realized what was happening, the little, old man
whisked me away to the back of the museum.

"I have an old pump organ that I want to show you," he
said.

I was intrigued.

"I want you to sit down and play it," he said firmly, yet lovingly. "The song is there on the ledger for you to play."

I looked at the small pump organ. The ledger held a very old
hymnal. It was opened to the hymn "Blessed Assurance." I sat
down. The nice man told me how to pump the organ.

"Pump each foot up and down, just like you're riding a
bicycle."

Following the man's instructions, I sat at the pump organ. I
held my sunglasses in my left hand and pitifully plunked out
the start of "Blessed Assurance" with my right hand. I only
made it through the first line when the little man interrupted
me saying, "No, no, not like that . . . you have to use both
hands! The bass on this organ is incredible!" The odd thing was,
I don't like to play piano for friends or strangers. *It's a long
story . . . but God's been working on me.*

Obediently, I set my sunglasses down. I began to play the
little pump organ with both hands and both feet. I was amazed
at the sound—it was incredible. I'm positive all of the Dows'

population could hear me play! It sounded so full, so beautiful. I finished that magnificent hymn and immediately said, "I have to get my husband. He'll never believe this."

I briskly walked outside to get Bruce. He wasn't too pleased that I awakened him, but I was excited. Hesitantly, he walked in with me, met the little, white-haired man with the twinkle in his eyes, and listened to me play "Blessed Assurance" on the pump organ—the whole thing, again! I left Dows feeling so peaceful and full of joy.

Was that an angel I just met in that little, old man? How did he know I could play the piano? And why was he so insistent that I play that song on the organ when he never asked any other visitors to play while I was there? Bruce was amazed at the transformation and giddiness in me. I told him I felt like we were meant to go to the Welcome Center for a greater purpose. I sensed that somehow it was in preparation for us to go to the healing crusade. *Actually, I secretively was waiting for someone to come out and tell me I was on candid camera and would be on the next episode of Little House on the Prairie and Laura and Pa would show up at any minute.*

Finally, we made it to my brother's home in Des Moines. I told my brother and his wife about my "Blessed Assurance" pump organ experience, and then off to the crusade we went. It was a wonderful time of prayer, praise, and worship, but the climax came when the speaker started singing favorite old hymns. He suddenly stopped right in the middle of a hymn medley. Interrupting everything, he said we couldn't continue until we sang his most favorite hymn—"Blessed Assurance"! Bruce and I looked at each other and laughed. With the orchestra resounding, hundreds of choir members, and more than 12,000 people in the auditorium, we stood and raised our voices to God and sang "Blessed Assurance." I guess God knew what we needed after all. We needed to hear of God's blessed assurance that He would always be with us, every step of the way in this journey we traveled.

It's just like God to speak to us in unconventional ways and to make something out of the nothingness in our lives. Through this experience I saw my life in a whole new light. Knowing that time is precious and no one knows the number of our days, except God, I now strive to live each day as if it's my last, and at the end of each day to know I've lived my best. While resting in the promises of God's blessed assurance, I will praise Him for these unique and special days!

• Chapter 12 •

Scraped Raw

The Wallpaper

I remember when Bruce and I bought our house. As with most houses, there are always things that need "fixing up." Either something is broken, the wrong color, showing wear and tear, or it's just not "you." Usually, in the remodeling process, we bite off more than we can chew. We begin tearing things apart to make them look better only to find more work and repairs that need to be done. Our simple little projects often take on lives of their own. We've had our share of projects that grew to gargantuan proportions. This time, the project was the wallpaper in the family room. It was falling off in spots, ripped, and really ugly. We both agreed that it needed to come down.

I was so proud of myself. I went to the wallpaper store, picked out some attractive wallpaper, bought the necessary supplies, and returned home. Pulling off the old wallpaper was the fun part. It came off easily, but it was messy. We washed the walls and prepared them for new wallpaper. The old glue needed to be removed, and the walls needed to be smooth. Smooth? No wonder the old wallpaper was falling off. The walls were anything but smooth. It was apparent they were never prepared properly. A bumpy, rough texture coated the walls. What were we to do now, and how were we supposed to remove the bumps?

We both went back to the wallpaper store and explained our dilemma. The best suggestion they could give us was to use a power sander or an old brick.

We took their ideas home. Bruce rigged up his power sander and began the grueling task of smoothing out the walls. After going through every grit of sandpaper, he burned out the motor to the power sander. Thankfully, we only needed to sand the upper-half of the walls. Wainscoting covered the bottom half. While Bruce was busy burning out motors on power tools, I scraped the walls with an old brick. The brick was working, but required extreme muscle power and a lot of hard work. Frankly, my motor was burning out too.

We worked and then worked some more. What started out to be a small, fun project became physically taxing and draining. Fine dust filled the air, and it was hard to breathe. Our muscles ached, and we were tired. After a lot of time and energy, we were able to smooth out all the jagged areas, and the walls were then properly prepared for the beauty that awaited them.

Thinking back to our little project, I saw a direct correlation between our lives and the wallpaper. Bruce and I were being stripped of every security and comfort to which we had grown accustomed. We were stripped of the security of knowing he had a job that would provide financially for our family. We thought that we'd grow old together, and he would always have good health. Even our security in knowing our children would have two parents throughout their lives was threatened.

Similar to the walls of our family room, we were being stripped, cleansed of our old self, and scraped of all our bumps and imperfections. Physical, emotional, and psychological blisters developed. The toil and turbulence was not over yet. Nothing in our life was secure. Like the brick scraping against the wall, our hearts were being scraped, and it hurt like nothing I've ever felt before. In the midst of this trial, we faced a choice. We could choose to endure the trials before us or whine and complain about it. It is often difficult to take the high road and grin and bear it, but we chose to take the high road. We knew there was nothing easy we could do to change our circumstances. Trials and suffering will do that to you. Both force you to choose.

The Dance Longed For

Bruce was looking forward to the upcoming weekend. He was supposed to be the best man for my brother Dale's wedding. The weekend before the wedding, Bruce started to get a cough. His chest was feeling tingly and tight. But in true fashion, he was thinking of others first, before himself. He walked into Parker Hughes with a surgical mask over his nose and mouth. He wasn't protecting himself from others and their germs. He was protecting others from himself, because he felt like he was coming down with something.

Of all people, Bruce knew chemo patients have a low immune system and can catch bacteria and viruses easily. The nurses and doctors all thought it was so sweet that Bruce would think of the other patients instead of himself. As you can imagine, they all liked him. Sure enough, after his doctor examined him and asked many questions, then listened to his lungs, we were sent to the radiologist to get a chest x-ray. Much to our surprise, he had bronchitis.

Our doctor immediately started Bruce on a potent intravenous antibiotic, and a peace pipe was strapped to his mouth to suck on. Actually, it was a nebulizer with medication that he breathed into his lungs. Having bronchitis in his weakened condition was nothing to take lightly. We had worked so hard to keep our family healthy, and with autumn here, we knew this was bound to happen sooner or later. We were thankful that God had granted us all good health until then.

The bronchitis diagnosis came at a very bad time. Within days we were supposed to travel with the kids and my mom to Eau Claire, Wisconsin, for Dale and Jayne's wedding.

The doctors knew how important this weekend was for Bruce, because he told everyone at the clinic that he needed to be well enough to dance with his wife at the wedding. It had been too long since our last dance. He told everyone that dancing was special to us and stemmed way back to when we fell in love at the eighteen-hour dance-a-thon in college. The doctors and nurses loved the dance story and were determined to do their best to make this dance a reality.

When my brother Dale asked Bruce to be the best man, it was May. November seemed to be such a long way away. Bruce told me that he was concerned he would not be able to stand up for my brother and may not even be here. That was a hard concept to swallow and one that he didn't dwell on too long. It was such an honor for him to be asked to be Dale's best man, and he was determined not to let cancer get in his way. My two brothers had become more than brother-in-laws to Bruce and visa versa. They were like real brothers in every sense of the word. Bruce prayed for months that God would protect him and make him well enough to stand up for Dale. In spite of his persistent prayers, he was about to face a few snags in the road. Not only would he get bronchitis right before the wedding, but also his platelet counts would plummet once again.

Even though Bruce received intravenous antibiotics for his bronchitis, the morning we were to leave town, his platelets crashed even lower. As soon as we got word of his low count, I took him to the hospital to get an emergency platelet transfusion. He was remarkable; again, only God's touch could have allowed him to do the things that were in store for us.

We made it to Eau Claire for the wedding. Bruce was able to stand for the entire ceremony—thirty-five minutes. This was totally unheard of, considering the cancer was in his vertebrae.

We danced at the reception! Then, he danced with his precious nine-year-old daughter, Nicole. She was dressed so prettily. He danced with my mom, the bride, then me again, and we danced all night. Bruce was at his best, and my heart was bursting all night with giddiness and glee to God for giving us our heart's desire. To me it seemed like a fairy tale night. Psalm 37:4 says, "Delight yourself in the Lord and he will give you the desires of your heart." Boy, did I delight in the Lord that night!

The Big Hunt

On the way home from the wedding, we received a call that Bruce's mom was taken by ambulance to a hospital only two hours from our home. She needed a pacemaker. Luckily, my mom was still with us from the wedding, and she agreed to stay a few extra days with the kids so we could be with Bruce's mom. The surgery was successful, and after a few days we returned home in time for Bruce to get ready to go deer hunting with his father, brother, nephew, and son, Blake. His mom stayed at our house so I could help her mend from her surgery.

I started to get concerned about Bruce, because the latest CT scan showed the cancer in his liver was more active. He began to feel new pain by his liver, and his abdomen became enlarged. The schedule had been crazy lately, and we agreed that he needed to slow down. He promised me that after the deer hunt he would concentrate on healing his body.

Bruce was an avid hunter. He dreamed of the day that he would be able to take his son on his first deer hunt. He even dreamed of taking his daughter too. Often, he told me that it wasn't all about "the hunt"; it was about being alone in nature. It was about clearing your head and just being quiet in God's creation. It didn't matter how cold it would get on those clear, crisp, early November mornings. Whether he saw a deer or not, there was joy in just watching the leaves fall to the ground and hearing them crunch under his boots as he quietly walked in the woods to his deer stand.

With the deer hunt, my brother's wedding, and Bruce's mom's time in the hospital, things were moving fast, and I could see the toll that it was taking on Bruce. God had seen to it that he would stand up as the best man for my brother's wedding, but would He be so generous as to grant this hunting desire too? Time was so precious these days.

The big hunt finally arrived. The best way to sum up the "male version" of the hunting story is to liken their hunting experience to fishing! I can relate to that, because I love to fish in the summer. You know how it goes when a group goes fishing—someone always gets the first, the most, the biggest, and so on. Well, this is the "fishing version" of the guy's hunting story. Chuck, Bruce's brother from Baton Rouge, Louisiana, got the first. Colin, our nephew and Chuck's son, got the biggest. Blake, our 13-year-old-son, was the youngest MacKenzie ever to shoot a deer. And Bruce cleaned up with the most! He ended up shooting two deer, giving one to his dad. It was the best hunt the MacKenzie boys ever had at the hunting shack. Bruce was in the hunting shack resting when Blake arrived at the cabin all excited. Bruce went to the door to see what all the commotion was about, and there stood Blake, beaming from ear to ear, with his first deer. Blake told me that night on the phone, "Mom, you wouldn't believe it, but Dad came to the door, saw me and the deer, and just started to cry!"

I silently prayed, *Thank you God for allowing your bountiful blessings in answer to yet another one of the desires of Bruce's heart.*

Bruce was completely exhausted after the exciting deer hunt. It had been more than six months of straight chemo, and I calculated that out of the previous twenty-eight days, he had been out of town for twenty—not a prescription for someone with Stage IV cancer. After the hunt, Bruce went into a deep, dark valley, which meant he was in a lot of pain, pretty much home bound and not bouncing back from the blue days he was experiencing. During that time we received a CD in the mail from a fifteen-year-old girl whom we didn't know. Her mom had been getting the e-mail updates and had shared our story with her daughter. She was so moved by our story that she asked her mom if they could send one of her favorite CD's to us. The CD was from the group *MaryMary*, and we were told to listen to the song "Can't Give Up Now." It was perfect timing, and the song was a great blessing to our family. The CD came at a very low point for us and helped us get back to trusting in the unseen when the walls seemed to be closing in on us.

The Tiring Walk

December arrived. With each turn of the calendar month, Bruce and I looked at each other and smiled. It was yet another month God had gifted us with. Per my request, Thanksgiving was spent quietly with just Bruce, Blake, Nicole, and myself. It was nice to have a low-key holiday considering all the activities that led up to Thanksgiving. Looking back, it was a wise decision, because Blake ended up getting strep throat and was the "Masked MacKenzie" over Thanksgiving. If one of us got sick, we had to wear a mask in the house until we were sure the bug had left. Blake was a real trooper and wore his mask at all times, except in his room. I, on the other hand, played referee to keep my boys at opposite ends of the house. Bruce still felt the effects of the triple chemo he received just before Thanksgiving. He never did come out of the valley-walk this time.

Bruce's cancer definitely became more active. His "tumor markers" went way up again, and his liver was enlarged. To be honest, this last round was tough on both of us. Maybe it was the holidays . . . maybe the road was just getting long . . . maybe it was getting bumpier . . . maybe we were just tired . . . or maybe there was just a truck load of pebbles in our shoes! Whatever the reasons, Bruce was going from one valley to the next this time. I seemed to be in my own valley.

Despite our valleys, we still counted our blessings and trudged on in the battle. One of the many blessings-in-disguise came right before we were to go to Parker Hughes and receive the news of all Bruce's test results. Before the appointment for the test results, I had been sensing a big nudge to journal our cancer journey. I periodically journal but have never been very consistent at it. The nudging I felt was beginning to get annoying, so the night before Bruce was to get chemo, I began to tippy-tap on the computer keys to journal. I decided to go back to the beginning of our journey, when we found out Bruce had cancer.

I wrote about the weekend leading up to the doctor visits and the test results that would forever change our lives. Whining to the computer keys about everyone forgetting my birthday, I suddenly found myself filled with remorse. Tears streamed down my face as I typed out a prayer asking God to forgive me for feeling sorry for myself that day, and I admitted my regrettable behavior. I should have been grateful for what I had and thankful for my blessings. Instead, I looked at the very blessings God gave me as curses. I felt like such a schmuck! I turned the computer off and went up to bed.

The next morning, Bruce got out of bed really early. At times he had trouble sleeping, so he'd go to the living room and snuggle up with his fleece blanket on his recliner, usually to fall back asleep. I didn't pay much attention that particular morning. I was tired from staying up late the night before and wanted to catch every moment of sleep I could that morning.

We were to leave for Parker Hughes and get the test results that day. Thankfully, Bruce started to walk out of the "chemo valley" the day before. The valley from chemo had definitely had its way with Bruce that time. I was just about to get up when Bruce came into the bedroom with a tray in his hands. On the tray was a plate with two eggs, bacon, toast, and hash browns. He was serving me breakfast in bed! I nearly cried. First of all, up until this time, Bruce just hadn't felt good enough to do anything, let alone cook. Secondly, no one knew that I had just typed the night before about not getting breakfast in bed on my birthday back in April, except God! Wow! Bruce said "the thought just came to him" that morning as he couldn't sleep anymore and he was getting hungry. I truly believe that was God's gracious way of letting us know that day that He was in control, He always has been in control, and He will continue to be in control! *Thank you, thank you, God.*

We could now face whatever news we were to receive that day knowing there was someone greater than us beside us all day—our Master Physician. We received a mixed bag of news. The good news was that the PET scan (which shows actual cancer activity) revealed that the cancer in Bruce's vertebrae, lung area, lymph nodes, ribs, and brain was pretty much inactive! No activity equals no cancer spread. We were so thankful and prayed that the sleeping cancer would go into a deeper coma, never to awaken again. The bad news was the PET scan revealed that the cancer was very active in Bruce's liver.

The CT scan revealed what originally appeared as many and varied-size spots on his liver were now a big connected blob. That explained the increased numbers in his tumor markers, enlarged liver, and increased pain. We were told that if we were unable to stop the growth and activity soon, Bruce would be in real trouble. The head of Parker Hughes said on a scale of 1 to 100 in regard to how concerned he was for Bruce—he was at a 99. That got our attention. We both felt like we received a few punches in the stomach that day, but our faith never wavered, because we knew who the unseen, Gentle Giant was in that room with us. That Gentle Giant had been with both of us since we woke up and enjoyed breakfast in bed!

Bruce was put on a strict diet—no meat, cheese, milk, or any dairy products. He had to eat the egg whites of six eggs each day! That was where he'd get his protein. Egg whites have a certain component rich in lecithin that aids the liver in digestion. I started juicing more fruits and vegetables. We were doing whatever we could to give his liver a break so it could concentrate on working on attacking the cancer instead of working so hard at filtering out foods.

The following week we returned for another check up and were scheduled to go to Fairview Hospital. Bruce needed a platelet transfusion so his counts would be high enough to allow him to get through surgery; he was going to have a *port* put in. This is minor surgery to insert a small object under the skin below his neck, in the chest area. The port has a catheter that is threaded into his heart. This makes access easier for all the chemo and blood draws. The doctors said they'd give Bruce until the end of this month to see a turnaround, or they might have to stop chemo treatments and put him on Iressa, which is a miracle drug for a small percentage, but not the majority. The FDA had not approved the drug, but Bruce had been approved to receive it on a "compassionate basis." He likened going on Iressa to throwing the "Hail Mary" in football.

It was then I was reminded of a card my brother Dean sent to me, which I quote: "In prayer, what matters is not the size of the mountain . . . but the strength of the mountain mover." I clung to those words.

• Chapter 13 •

A New Year

The Christmas Gift

Christmas was wonderful. We spent Christmas Eve and Christmas at Bruce's sister, Kyle's house. The next weekend we went to my mom's, and the entire Drevlow family gathered for a belated Christmas celebration. The entire holiday season was momentous, but something special happened on Christmas Day.

The whole MacKenzie clan gathered around the Christmas tree in the living room. Bruce read the Christmas story out of the Bible from the book of Luke. Each family member was given a candle to hold and told to tell of a significant event that happened during that year to them or something that they were thankful for and then to share their hopes and dreams for the New Year. As each person shared, they lit their candle. When all finished, we blew out the candles. One by one, family members shared. Blake, Nicole, and I were some of the last to share. What pierced my heart the most was what my two children said and how they weren't too afraid to be honest.

Individually, they told the family that no child ever dreams their dad will get such a horrible disease as cancer. It was something that had changed their lives forever. They spoke of the blessings in the sufferings. They said it wasn't easy going through this. They testified how proud they were of their dad and mom and the sharing of our faith with the family to keep them strong daily. They thanked God for the family He gave them and prayed for complete healing in the New Year so their dad could get back to being the dad they used to have and be able to continue to serve God in whatever way God wanted.

I could barely speak when my turn came. My tear faucet was wide open. Bruce and I were both so proud of our children and the courage they displayed by sharing what had weighed heavily on their precious young hearts. No present under the tree could have compared to the gift we were given as parents through the honesty of our children that afternoon.

It's amazing how our adult sufferings affect our children. Never give up on your children, parents! They'll amaze you someday with the wonderful truths they have learned from you, and someday you'll get caught off guard with your tear faucet wide open too. Proverbs 22:6 says, "Train a child in the way he should go, and when he is old he will not turn from it."

The Great Anticipation

New Years is always anticipated and celebrated in various ways by different people. For many it's an excuse to party until wee hours of the morning on New Years Eve and then stay in your pajamas and watch football games all day on New Years Day. For others, it's just more of the same old grind, and they grumble all through the party while they channel surf to find something other than happy people on the television.

Our New Years seemed to be a combination of thankfulness, great expectations, and uncertain dreads. As many people do on New Years, I reflected on the previous year. A new year was right around the corner, and even though I was thankful to have reached this destination, I was scared. The cancer was incurable, the fight was wearing on us, and time was so precious.

The New Year's Dream

Over New Years, Bruce felt great. We had purchased a new TV with surround sound for our family room after saving up for years. The old TV was mine from college. We had talked about getting a new one for years, and with Bruce home and spending a great deal of time in front of the TV, this Christmas season seemed to be the ideal time to purchase one.

On New Years Eve day, Bruce recruited Blake to help him set up the TV and surround sound. They worked all afternoon, and I worried that Bruce was overdoing it. Occasionally, I'd go down to the family room to check on them. The family room was a sea of boxes, paper, parts, and instruction sheets. He assured me that he was fine and preferred that I go upstairs and continue doing what I was doing—whatever that was. It was obvious that I was only making him nervous, and he wanted to be left alone with his son.

Our New Years tradition had been to spend time with our neighbors, the Scofields. This year would be no different. Even though Bruce was on a no-protein diet, he decided to splurge for supper. We made reservations at our favorite little restaurant called *Friends Bar and Grill.* They had a New Years crab special. Crab is one of my favorite foods, and through the years I eventually got Bruce to love the little pink legs. He told me that he was tired of finishing his main course of food and then sitting there watching me eat crab for another hour.

Cherie began to love the little morsels too. I remember the first time she ordered crab, and I needed to teach her how to "crack" the shell. She was patiently learning, and I dubbed her a very good "crab cracking" student. I taught her the art of getting the succulent pieces of crabmeat out of the shells while keeping the meat intact. Only then could you dip it in the drawn butter with lemon juice squirted in it. It truly was an art. Cherie was now on her own in the "crab cracking" business. She was concentrating and diligently working at her crab when all of a sudden, I picked up one of the crab claws from my plate. While moving the crab pinchers up and down and speaking in a small voice I said, "Hi Cherie, how are you doing?"

She looked up at me and laughed. Her face grimaced in a way that seemed to be challenging me in my playfulness, and she grabbed one of the crab claws on her plate. Moving them up and down and speaking in a small voice she said, "Fine. I'm just fine. How are you?" By now, Bruce and Cherie's husband, Alan, were looking at each other as if to say, "Do you know them? I don't." Ah, the memories of New Years past.

After the crab feast, we always returned to the Scofield's house to play cards. We loved playing the card game *Phase 10*, and with a fire roaring in the fireplace and a card table next to it, we played cards until the wee hours of the morning. Alan had put in the movie *Remember the Titans* to watch during our card game. Bruce was absolutely enthralled with it. Midnight came and went, and he was at his best. At some point the kids came bounding downstairs to bring in the New Year with us. We had been oblivious to the time.

At 1:20 A.M. I told Cherie I thought Bruce was completely healed but just keeping it to himself. He was acting almost normal! When 2:30 A.M. arrived, Cherie and I were really dragging our wagons. Bruce was wide-eyed and bushy-tailed and full of energy. He kept clicking the remote control for the TV/DVD to watch all the out-takes from *Remember the Titans*. After prompting and prodding, he agreed to wake our sleeping children, walk next door to our house, and put them in their own beds. The snow and crispness of the cold winter air was biting, yet invigorating. It was a clear night, and the moon was full and brilliant. There was no need for flashlights. The moonlight illuminated the path between our homes, and everything around us seemed so alive. It's amazing how beautiful the wintry white is in the stillness of the early morning hours.

Hand in hand with Bruce, I asked him a question I'll never forget. I said, "You're not faking feeling good for my sake are you?" Of course, the minute those words came out of my mouth I knew how silly that question was.

Bruce replied, "No! Do you think I could even begin to fake something like that . . . I feel great!"

"You're right," I said, and then arm-in-arm we walked into our warm home. After putting the kids to bed and getting ready for bed ourselves, Bruce still seemed for a brief moment to be just fine. No cancer. No illness. Nothing. It was almost as if I actually did wake up from this dreadful dream, only I knew that wasn't the truth. It was simply another gift from God.

During that night, I had an incredible experience. I laid my head on Bruce's chest and rested in his arms. I hadn't laid my head on his chest for months, because he usually hurt everywhere from the cancer. After we prayed together, I snuggled in for the night with a smile on my face. I was so happy. As I was sleeping, I had a dream or saw something like a vision. I know one thing for sure—it was of God! In my sleep and all through the night I worshipped and sang praises to God like I've never done before. I'd wake briefly many times and hear the song *Worthy is the Lamb* flood through my head and heart. Sometime during the night, I seemed to have an out-of-body experience. You know, like you see on TV where someone is having surgery and they come out of their body and can watch the surgeons working on them while they look down from above. I did that. I was above the bed looking down at Bruce and myself peacefully sleeping.

It was dark in the room as we slept, but covering us was what looked like a coating of powdery, pure white snow, only the snow wasn't cold. It wasn't even really snow. It was perfect. It was so white, and in my soul I felt a peace like I've never felt before. I also felt comfort and knew it had something to do with healing. The whole experience didn't last long; it was like God was showing me something. But what was it?

Later that night I had another experience, only this time I was in the bed looking up. Above the covers hovered what looked like a coiled, fuzzy pipe cleaner. It was coiled over the entire bed in a coil similar to a space heater's, yet it never touched the bed or us. It was clear, with a soft blue tint to it. It almost appeared to have a calming warm glow. Again, I felt an incredible sense of peace and protection. I also had a sense that somehow this had to do with healing. I awoke that morning feeling great, and praise songs continued to resonate all day in my head. I told Bruce about the dream, and he just smiled. What a neat way to start the New Year. For days I wondered what this dream meant. I wanted to know. Whatever it was seemed like a foretelling of things to come.

The Mouse Chase

It was the end of January, and the cold and flu viruses were trying their best to worm their way into our home. Nicole was running a low-grade temperature and felt achy. I put her to bed with Kleenex, a glass of water, a towel, and a pail. Then it was Blake's turn to be put to bed. He brushed his teeth, and I prayed him up (our usual routine). After he prayed, with a smile on my face, I said to him, "Did you hear that? It sounded like BoTie was going wild!" BoTie had gone out to the garage. Blake soon went out to the car to get his backpack. He was completely unaware that BoTie sneaked back into the house when he returned from the garage.

I left Blake's room and went down to the dining room area to see what BoTie was up to. She was by the piano and had something in her mouth. She was flinging it to and fro. It wasn't a toy but a mouse, and it wasn't dead. I screamed for Bruce, but he was fast asleep downstairs on the couch. Poor guy, I felt so bad, but I didn't know what else to do. BoTie ran downstairs with the mouse in her mouth only to release it for a crazy adventure.

Blake emerged from his room to see what all the commotion was about. He immediately grabbed a broom from the closet. Bruce was awake by this time and was calling out to BoTie . . . "BoTie, get the mouse; good kitty, get the mouse."

This continued for some time. BoTie was excited, but she eventually lay down on the carpet as if to say, "I've done my work for the night, now it's your turn." Needless to say, she was not scoring brownie points with Bruce and Blake. I, on the other hand, stood guard at the top of the steps should BoTie or the mouse retreat to the main level. I shut all the doors I could think of in the house and found one of Blake's school science projects that was displayed on a large cardboard tri-fold. I used it to deter BoTie and the mouse in case they raced up the stairs for any reason. This was a stretch for me, I'll have you know, and I was praying the whole time.

The mouse went behind the entertainment center . . . then the couch . . . then the entertainment center . . . then by the stairs . . . then behind the couch . . . then up on the ledge above the couch . . . Blake started whacking the broom at it about that time. Then it scurried under the entertainment center. I was the look out. Blake and Bruce had a broom, yard stick, flashlight, or a hammer in one or both of their hands. Occasionally that darn 'ol mouse would just take off. BoTie would catch it once in a while, and we'd be so proud, only to release it and let the chase begin again! Finally, Bruce eyeballed the mouse behind the entertainment center, and he stabbed it with his broom! He called Blake over to get the fireplace tongs and reach under him to grab the mouse that was being held prisoner under his broom. It was so comical . . . everyone was yelling, and the poor mouse was history. Blake was about to finally squeeze under his dad to secure the mouse in the tongs, when BoTie proudly moseyed up to the dead mouse and sniffed it. "Yep, that's the one; good job guys."

Bruce collapsed on the couch after that hunting experience. I've often wondered why that unusual event happened. Frankly, I found the whole ordeal hilarious. Here we were in the dull drones of winter; all the while, life continued around us, and there was really nothing to laugh at.

I'm sure BoTie was tired of all the sick people in our house, sulking around, waiting for spring to arrive. BoTie just thought she'd throw us a little diversion to stir things up a bit. She must have thought the mouse hunt would get them to stop sulking.

Of course, BoTie made sure when she caught the mouse that she wouldn't kill it. She did her best to conceal it. Then when no one was looking, she unclenched her jaw, and released the mouse. I'm sure in her warped kitty mind she heard the bell ding twice, and an imaginary referee robustly announce, "Let the games begin."

Chapter 14

Questioning this Path

The Fear

Valentines Day, like New Years Day, can be filled with a wide variety of emotions for different people. If you have someone you love in your life, then Valentines Day is a special day. If you just broke up or haven't found Mr. or Mrs. Right, then Valentines Day can be painful. This year Valentine's Day conjured up many emotions. Bruce and I were definitely in love, but the kind of love we were experiencing was in the "for better or worse" stage. Honestly, it was in the "for worse" stage. I felt Bruce slowly slipping away from me, and I was getting scared.

Over the years we had celebrated many special Valentines Days. On our ten-year wedding anniversary, we spent the day alone on the island of Maui. One year we traveled on Valentines Day with our kids to Disney World. The Disney World trip was amazing. We always wanted to take our kids there but financially it seemed impossible. Then Bruce had a business conference in Orlando, Florida, in February. His plane ticket, the hotel, and rental car would be covered; it appeared to be a no-brainer, and the kids and I flew down to join him at the end of the conference. That was two months before his cancer was discovered. It was a wonderful time, with just the four of us. During the Florida trip, Bruce had several dizzy spells and bouts of not feeling well. Looking back, it was apparent that the metastasis in his brain began to impair normal living. We often talked about the timing of the trip and how just two months later we would find out that Bruce had cancer.

A few months earlier we had driven down to Orange Beach, Alabama, to spend Christmas with the entire MacKenzie family. We spent seven days on the beach and created beautiful memories. God knew Bruce would get cancer, and He knew exactly when it would be discovered. We both realized that God had given us quality family time before we ventured down the cancer path. We saw the coincidences of those two big trips as no coincidence. God was not only present when we learned of "the news," but also He was preparing us months before.

The path now seemed to be curving, and I wasn't sure where it was going. Physically, Bruce seemed to be doing better. Inwardly, I felt a change. It was almost as if the light surrounding me was growing dim.

The cat and mouse chase added an unexpected twist in the humdrum routine of "walking in the valley of the shadow of chemo," and so would some of the events that followed. Just when we thought we had gone through all the firsts of cancer, something else was staring us in the face. The events were often subtle, but it made us stop and think about the road we were heading down. The terrain was changing, and we asked ourselves if God was giving us time to prepare for something bigger.

The Emergency Room

Valentines Day came and went, and Bruce continued being faithful with his new diet of no protein. He was regimented about eating six egg whites each day. I started to think I needed to purchase a few of my own chickens; I never seemed to have enough eggs.

Bruce went back to work for approximately four hours per week. It may not seem like a thimble's worth of work to most people, but for him that was all he could take. Chemo continued almost weekly, and he waffled among feeling yucky, okay, or sort of good. "Great" wasn't on the radar since New Years. But we were thankful for seeing the New Year, and now we waited upon the Lord.

One Wednesday in February, I was getting ready to go to my weekly Bible study. Before I left, Bruce told me about a new strange pain he periodically felt over his heart and told me he was going to call his oncologist. The pain had kept him awake since 4 A.M. He didn't complain much, considering all he'd been put through, so when he complained and felt the need to inform his doctor, I took notice. Because he was going to have chemo the next day, he thought they might want to update the EKG/ECHO cardiogram. He called Parker Hughes and amazingly reached the head of Parker Hughes. After he learned of Bruce's symptoms, he urgently told him to do two things: take an aspirin and get to the emergency room. Bruce's type of cancer, compiled with the months and months of chemo, put him at a much higher risk for heart problems and/or plural embolisms, which are blood clots.

Meanwhile, after my Bible study, I went to lunch at a Chinese restaurant with three wonderful friends. Suddenly, the manager walked among the patrons and said, "Lynn MacKenzie?" I raised my hand like some schoolgirl, and he handed me the phone. It was Bruce: I needed to come home right away and take him to the emergency room because of his chest pain. He said that if I couldn't get home soon he'd have to call the ambulance. Wow, that hit me in the gut like a rocket. Tears began as I shook my head up and down and muff 'ed out that I'd come home right away.

My friends watched and waited until I told them what happened. My friend Teri asked to pray quickly before we left. We did. She ended her prayer by asking for this to be a false alarm and for us to have God's peace. They called others to pray for Bruce. Jennifer drove me back to my car. She asked, "Are you okay to drive home, Lynn?"

I looked at her, smiled, and said, "I'll be okay, Jen; I can see through my tears . . ." I recalled saying that one other time.

Thankfully, Paul Froland was at home with Bruce at the time. As I drove up to the house, I saw Bruce sitting on a chair in the middle of our living room, and Paul had his hands on Bruce. *They must be praying,* I thought.

As I drove to the emergency room, Bruce and I called everyone we could think of to pray for us. Because of that precious prayer in the restaurant, I was able to focus on looking up. We weren't going to rely on the emergency room doctors and nurses, but the greatest Physician of them all! Our pastor even met us in the emergency room and prayed with us.

I won't bore you with the details, but through blood tests, oxygen, an EKG, a chest x-ray, and a CT scan, the doctors ruled out the worst possible scenario. No heart problems, no blood clots. They never really did figure out the origin of the pain he felt that day. They wrote it off as muscle spasms in his chest wall. We were relieved to be finished with this chapter in our journey, but you can bet I let Bruce know he had crossed the ER bridge, and he never needed to go back over it again! I even teased that he seemed to be going for every medical experience possible on this journey. The only bridge he hadn't crossed yet was a hospital stay, and I didn't want him going there!

The Deaths

Was it preparation or was it just a coincidence? Death and dying seemed to be surrounding us. In all my life I'd never encountered so many people that Bruce and I knew who were sick or had just died. Death didn't respect age, occupation, or religion, and it appeared in many forms.

I remember one night feeling so overcome with emotions, wonderment, and a sense of seeing "the big picture" that I sat down and typed the following journal entry. I've deliberately left off last names in respect to their families. What astonished me was the number of deaths, types of deaths, and ages of these loved people. The bottom line; death had many faces, and it seemed to be closing in on us.

> Yesterday marked the fourth funeral Bruce and I attended in the past five months. For many others, we paid our respects at the funeral home or sent cards. Eleven of our friends died in the last five months. Three were people that attended Bruce's prayer and healing service in June.

> *John* died suddenly of complications from surgery after having his stomach stapled. John was one of the people with a spatula in his hand, flipping burgers at Bruce's benefit.

> *Dolores* came to our Prayer and Healing service with her husband, Dick. She was diagnosed with a rare form of leukemia in October. Due to complications from a fungus that formed in her lungs, she passed away right before Christmas.

> *Richard,* a sweet, older man that we knew from our church, died from complications of a stroke and fall.

Dennis died from cancer right after the hunting season. I was shocked one day at Parker Hughes when I saw Dennis was getting chemo right next to Bruce. The ironic thing was that his wife, Nancy, and I used to work together many years ago. What a small world.

John, one of our best friend's brother, died from cancer too. John had melanoma.

Yesterday, we attended the funeral for our friend's father. *Hollis* died from a massive heart attack while hunting in Mexico.

Tonight I received a call from my Bible Study Fellowship leader to inform me that one of our group member's *brother* was killed in a farm machinery accident. Barb had just lost her *dad* before Christmas in a farm accident also. Her brother was trying to help his mom on the farm when the accident happened. He had recently moved back home. His young life ended tragically.

Bruce also befriended a gentleman from Wisconsin who had the same cancer as Bruce. His name was *Daniel.* He was Bruce's age and he had three young children. Bruce met him over the phone through mutual acquaintances. They immediately hit it off. They also shared the same grounded faith. They spoke often on the phone and followed each other's cancer progress, cheering each other on in the fight and sharing spiritual matters. I'll never forget

when Daniel was knocking on Heaven's door.
Bruce spoke to him only days before he died.
Bruce was so anxious in the days after that
conversation. When he received the call that
Daniel had finally met his Savior, Bruce saw his
own mortality in a new way.

When Bruce and I decided to go to Parker
Hughes Cancer Treatment Center, my mom
spoke several times of a cancer victim named
Joanie. She was only given a two-week prognosis
before transferring her treatment to the doctors
at Parker Hughes. That was two years ago. She
was one of the miracle stories that encouraged
us to go to Parker Hughes. Eventually, the
cancer would claim her life too.

Another Parker Hughes success story came
from a local gal named *Lisa.* I talked to Lisa
the night before we made our first visit to
Parkers Hughes. We even ran into her several
times while getting chemo treatments, talked
over the phone, and corresponded via e-mail.
Like Joanie, Lisa died after a long battle with
cancer.

The suddenness of these deaths only confirmed
our mortality here on earth. Time is so precious. Death is the end for those left behind.
But for the Christian, it's only the beginning of
the new life we have in Jesus. It's apparent that
we can't take anything with us. I have to ask
myself why I tend to get so caught up in the
business of the day and acquiring things.

The Tests

Every two months, Bruce had a big test week followed by consultation the following week. It was that time again. Early in the week, he was given a CT scan, brain MRI, PET scan (which shows "hot spots" of current cancer activity), and blood work to track tumor marker activity.

Later in the week, we went back to get more potent chemo drugs. It was our own personal "liquid gold." Toward the end of that afternoon, our oncologist danced into our little cubical. She grinned from ear to ear and jumped up and down while holding a piece of paper in her hands. Shaking it gleefully, she sang, "I've got good news . . . I've got good news!" She had just received the CT scan over the fax. *How could this be?* I thought. *It was just yesterday Bruce had the test—it's never done this soon!* The good news was that the cancer in the liver was getting smaller! Not only were there fewer lesions, but also they were significantly smaller.

Our doctor said, "Look Brucie," as she fondly called him, "it says s-i-g-n-i-f-i-c-a-n-t-l-y!" Then she underlined *significantly*. The largest tumor in his liver had shrunk from 6.3 cm. to 4.4 cm. since December. Praise God! That is a large drop in size. The scan showed the fluid around the lungs unchanged, and the cancer in the lungs was quiet.

Later that day, our oncologist met us a second time, and she was dancing again! This time she had the results of Bruce's tumor markers. She reported that they were as low as they've ever been since last summer! We praised God all the way home from Parker Hughes that day. We weren't supposed to know any results for one week, so we were twice as thankful to not have the wait.

The next night, at 10:40 P.M., our phone rang. Our phone usually doesn't ring past 10:00 P.M. I felt a pit in my gut. I answered the phone, and much to my surprise, it was the head of Parker Hughes on the phone.

He asked, "Is this Lynn?"

"Yes."

"Well, I'm sorry it's so late, but I was wondering if Bruce was still up."

Immediately, I ran downstairs to give Bruce the phone. Dr. Uckun called because he had just received Bruce's PET scan results and was so excited he had to call in person, right away.

The PET scan showed that the activity level of his cancer was next to nil. Two months prior, the scan lit up like a Christmas tree with major activity. Now, it was barely active. Another big praise to our majestic God! I told Dr. Uckun that he made our day. This was great news—one week early!

The next week we returned to Parker Hughes for more chemotherapy and the big consultation. By this time, there was nothing to consult about. It tickled the very base of my soul. When we first started doctoring at Parker Hughes, our oncologist seemed to gravitate toward Bruce and me. She would sit down with us at various times to discuss spiritual matters. She had gone from doubting and having real trouble with organized religion, to engaging in more and more conversation, then joining a church and rejoicing with us, even in our sufferings.

During the consult, she showed us on paper the test result and scans, and all while I kept saying, "Praise God, Praise God." With a big smile on her face, she put her hand on Bruce's knee and blurted out, "I just love God!" Then she said, "Brucie, you may just be our next Miracle Boy!"

Cool!

The plan was for Bruce to continue with the same chemo drugs for the next two months. No need to change something that was finally working, although we believed it was God at work, not the drugs. We were able to persuade our oncologist to hold off giving Bruce the drug *Temador*, which was that nasty oral chemo drug for his brain metastasis. The MRI of his brain showed no metastasis, and this was the second one that showed the cancer there was clear. They would do another MRI in six weeks and would reevaluate at that time. The other tests would be given again in two months.

I reminded Bruce that the next round of tests would be right before Easter, and in my boldness while praying to God, I mentioned that it would be a great time to completely heal him. I reminded God that it was around Easter time when He called my dad to his heavenly home; maybe He could display His glory and miraculously heal Bruce so that he could stay here on earth awhile longer. The tests would tell.

Ever since New Years, I'd had such an incredible peace. Even in our sufferings and trials, we are to thank God and praise Him. Since New Years, Bruce and I had shifted our prayer life. We were thanking and praising God for the opportunities that accompanied the cancer. For the blessings in the suffering, for the doors it opened, and the opportunities to meet so many needy people who lost all hope and couldn't see beyond their hurt and pain. We would never have been able to share God's love and matters of the heart with complete strangers if Bruce didn't have cancer. We thanked God for that. Psalm 40:1–4 says, "I waited patiently for the Lord; he turned to me and heard my cry. He lifted me out of the slimy pit, out of the mud and mire; he set my feet on a rock and gave me a firm place to stand. He put a new song in my mouth, a hymn of praise to our God. Many will see and fear and put their trust in the Lord."

Sometimes we can change our circumstances when trouble comes, but many times we can't. It's during those times I cling to and pray Psalm 40:1–4.

Chapter 15

Churning Waters

The Natural Disasters

The East Coast, specifically the Florida area, had been hit with multiple hurricane whip lashings. Shortly after the hurricanes pulverized the beautiful Florida and Gulf Shores coasts, the greatest tsunami of the century wrecked havoc on eleven countries in South Asia. Historians said it was one of the worst natural disasters our world has ever seen.

What once looked like a piece of heaven on earth now lay barren, full of scattered debris, and even the topography was permanently changed in many places. The weather anomaly forever affected thousands of lives. People were defenseless and had absolutely no control over their circumstances. How ironic as we compare weather changes with changes in our lives. Just as the water in our earth's oceans churned, so began the waters in the great sea of our lives. Only weeks earlier, everything was going so well. It was the calm before the storm. Soon our circumstances would change and form a new landscape. As I reflected on the similarities, I couldn't help but ask myself, *If I'm not in control of these seismic changes in the weather or in my life, then who is in control?* The answer was simple—God. Even though I felt out of control, I needed to trust in the One who was in control.

Somehow that conclusion gave me a strange comfort.

The Tide Turns

On March 4th, a sunny, cloudless morning greeted us. The sun was radiant, and the morning breeze was gently whispering that spring would soon arrive. The snow had turned into dirt-stained piles, and grass blades were desperately trying to peer through the winter's mat. Bruce took a long shower that morning. When he finished, we were once again on the road to Parker Hughes for another chemo treatment. We were entering the eleventh month of continuous chemotherapy treatments.

In our normal fashion, we stopped at McDonald's for a sausage egg McMuffin meal. Bruce only ordered the McMuffin with the egg. He was so loyal to his "no protein" diet, except for the six egg whites per day. On chemo days he would make an exception, and he would eat the entire egg. Once we made our breakfast pit stop, it was back on the highway for the sixty-mile drive.

As we drove to Parker Hughes, Bruce told me something that happened while he was in the shower that morning. He apologized for taking extra time to get ready, but said he spent most of it crying out to God. As the water ran down his tired body in the shower, so did the tears. He told God how tired he was. He had obviously put up a good front for all of us. But he was tired of chemo, he was tired of never really feeling good anymore, and he was simply tired of the fight. "When will this road end?" he cried out in tears of frustration and anguish, seeking relief from something beyond his control. I thanked him for his honesty and assured him not to worry about his additional shower time.

Once we arrived at the clinic, we were put in an area where three other men were receiving chemo. All four wives lovingly surrounded their husbands. In a funny way, we were all becoming good friends. Jerry, one of the men in our cubicle, was celebrating his 60th birthday. All the nurses went together to get him a beautiful sheet cake. Everyone was jovial and having a good time. We sang happy birthday to Jerry, cut the cake, and whoever wanted to participate in the celebration did so.

There was so much activity happening in our little cubicle that I barely noticed the nurse watching Bruce's chemo drip. She became alarmed. His oxygen level suddenly dropped, and she immediately stopped the drip. A flurry of nurses entered our cubical. One nurse brought over an oxygen tank and placed a mask on Bruce's face. I didn't understand what was happening. Others were still celebrating and conversing. They weren't aware he was in trouble. He started to cough and cough hard. Soon he was coughing up blood. He was scared. The fear was evident in his eyes. My heart raced and I felt helpless.

The internist came quickly and examined Bruce. Within minutes an appointment was made to get a chest x-ray at a nearby clinic. Bruce stood up to leave for the x-ray and almost fell over. He was light-headed and weak. Several nurses grabbed a wheelchair and moved quickly to help him get into our car. I put the car in reverse, backed up, and sped off.

I remember feeling so alone. I knew this was serious. We arrived at the clinic within minutes, and an x-ray was taken immediately. We waited while the films were developed; we needed to take them back with us. The look on the technician's face when she handed me the x-rays spoke volumes.

"Good luck," she simply said.

We returned to Parker Hughes, and Dr. Shafiq took me back to view the x-rays. He said it appeared to be a sudden onset of pneumonia. He recommended Bruce be admitted to the hospital for 48 hours to receive intravenous antibiotics. *48 hours . . . we could do that.* Suddenly I found myself remembering another time we "thought" Bruce may have had pneumonia. It turned out to be cancer. What would this chain of events turn out to be? I found myself feeling like I did in our early days of this journey. The air was heavy, the tears were accumulating, and I felt a panic settle at the core of my soul.

The tide had turned. I feared for our lives.

The Baton Is Passed

Before I realized what was happening, I had to stop sending out e-mails—at least for some time. But God in his grace would see to it that the message and updates continued, and Paul Froland grabbed the baton from me and made sure Bruce's Prayer Warriors received continual updates. He ran the rest of the race. The following are some excerpts from several of Paul's first e-mails to Bruce's Prayer Warriors:

> This note comes to you with a bit of urgency about Bruce. I spoke to Lynn earlier this evening, and Bruce was being admitted to Fairview University Hospital in the Cities. Bruce was battling a cold the past week, and they determined that it was the start of pneumonia. Bruce was having difficulty breathing with the pneumonia, and with the use of only one good lung, the doctors felt it was best to admit him and observe him for 48 hours.

> I would ask that you continue to stand in the gap for Bruce, lifting him to the Father, seeking healing and protection, and for the Lord to give Bruce His strength to fight off the pneumonia. . . . Bruce and Lynn's daughter, Nicole, told her mom and dad not to worry for there were angels at Parker Hughes, there were angels at the hospital, and there were angels in St. Cloud

with the kids, keeping a bubble of protection around all of them.

Updates continued in the remaining days.

The Hospital Stay

At 8:30 P.M. on March 4th, we entered the emergency doors to Fairview University Hospital in Minneapolis. Admissions checked Bruce in, and we were taken to a room on the seventh floor. Suddenly the world seemed big and intimidating. The hospital stay would be a living nightmare for us; it was unfamiliar, unfriendly, and very unfair.

I stayed overnight with Bruce the first night; he was scared and wanted me with him. Our children were well taken care of by our neighbors. *After all, we were told we were only going to be in the hospital for two days.* Over the course of the next few days, tests were taken, two or three different antibiotics were dripped into Bruce's veins, and he struggled to breathe.

Forty-eight hours turned into "just a few more days," and then we started to count the weeks. By then, my mom came to stay at our house and take care of our children. Each night I prayed that God would direct me as to when or if I should go home to be with my children. They were frightened being so far away from both of us, but I knew it was more important for me to stay with Bruce.

Through wonderful friends, we arranged for Blake and Nicole to come for short visits. Each time they came, it became harder and harder for them to say goodbye to us. With each new visit more machines were added to Bruce's room. The doctors were baffled as to why he was not responding to the antibiotics. They scheduled an endoscopy. Bruce was sedated, and the pulmonologist inserted a flexible tube down Bruce's throat to look inside his good lung. After the procedure the doctor visited with Kyle and me in the waiting room.

"It doesn't look good," she said. "Bruce has an alveolar hemorrhage, which means the alveoli in his lungs are bleeding. They are not supposed to. Steroids may help, but I'm very doubtful." Her assessment was devastating.

During the first ten days of his hospital stay, Bruce and I talked about everything. We discussed the "what ifs," and Bruce accepted whatever was ahead of him; however, he wasn't ready to give up yet and still wanted to fight. He wasn't ready to go, to say good bye for now.

I recalled when my dad was nearing the end of his earthly life, and we were alone. Out of the blue he said to me, "It's just so hard to say goodbye." I'm sure that's exactly how Bruce was feeling.

In the course of the hospital stay, Bruce progressively went from the "nose canulla" to the full-face oxygen mask, and then to the bi pap mask. He was told that the bi pap mask was like sticking your head out the window of a train as it was going 70 miles per hour. Each step was one more toward the final and the only choice left—the ventilator.

Days went by; snow fell and even melted as the world carried on with its routine. Every breath for Bruce became a chore. He had already changed rooms six times and received daily blood transfusions, pokes, and tests. Visitors came and went, people sent cards, they called, and all were sad to hear about the turning tide.

I stayed at Kyle and John's when I wasn't at the hospital. It became my home away from home, and I was so thankful for that blessing. One night, as I arrived at Kyle's after leaving the hospital, her phone rang. It was the nurse. Bruce had just coughed up an unusually large amount of blood. He was scared and wanted me to return. I was devastated after the call. Afraid for Bruce, I wanted desperately to be with him. Kyle and John were great; they didn't think twice about what to do. Kyle told me to get in the passenger seat of my car, and she'd drive my van to the hospital. John followed in their car. By the time we arrived, Bruce had settled down somewhat. The nurse was able to give him something for his agitation and anxiety. I stayed with him that night. Bruce told me that after I arrived he felt better. He said that my presence gave him great comfort and strength. What precious words they became in the days ahead. Bruce rallied that night, but only temporarily.

The next day he struggled again, and it was apparent that Bruce needed twenty-four hour nursing care. The floor he was on couldn't afford the staffing for proper care, and the nurses suspected that soon he would need the ventilator. The next evening after midnight, he would be transferred to ICU. Again, we received a phone call from the hospital at Kyle's house, and we immediately drove back to the hospital in the middle of the night. This was becoming an unsettling routine.

All Alone

The Ventilator

The road Bruce traveled now was getting to me. He struggled with every breath and was completely exhausted. Many family members came to see him one particular weekend. It was incredibly strenuous for him to concentrate and carry on a conversation. Even in ICU he was getting worse. The mood was somber, and it felt like those visiting came to say goodbye.

After everyone left Sunday night, we discussed our limited options with the night nurse. The bi-pap oxygen mask that Bruce was on wasn't meeting his needs. Although Bruce was conscious with the mask, the fight was more than he could bear. We were told that it would be better and easier for him physically if he made the decision to go on the ventilator instead of facing an emergency situation when the ventilator would need to be forced upon him.

Before I left that night, I told Bruce that I supported whatever decision he needed to make. I knew how hard he struggled and fought to breathe. He was so tired. I thanked him for fighting so hard and reminded him that God would take care of him, no matter what. He need not worry about us, but concentrate on himself.

Bruce pulled the bi-pap mask away from his face. With trembling hands on each side of my face, he began to lovingly and gently draw my face towards his, and he softly kissed me. With tears in his eyes and my face close to his, he quietly whispered, "I love you so much, Lynn." Then he paused and again he said, "No, I really love you, Lynn, and I always will." I kissed him back, and then looked in his tired eyes one last time. In the same fashion he had spoken to me I said, "I love you too, honey. I'll love you forever." Then I added, "Do what you have to do and know that the kids and I will be fine."

Kyle and I left with much trepidation. A long and narrow tunnel led to the hospital parking ramp. Somewhere halfway into the tunnel we decided to call Bruce's nurse. We had a question.

The question soon became irrelevant. Bruce's nurse told Kyle that he had already asked about the procedure of inserting the ventilator. Then he asked to be left alone for a few minutes. The nurse moved over to work on the computer in his room. During his alone time, he prayed. After a few minutes, he asked to be put on the ventilator. In Bruce's true fashion, he made one last important decision to spare me from making it. It was his last gift to me. I thanked God for that often.

The lights were dimming, and I struggled to see. My husband was alive, but now our communication was only one way. I could communicate with him, but he was so heavily sedated that not even a hand squeeze could be reciprocated.

I felt alone in a whole new way, and so I prayed:

> Father God, please hear me. Father God, please carry me. When I am weak, may you be strong. When I feel like crumbling, may you be the glue that holds me together. You know my heart Lord. You feel my pain. I don't profess to know your mind nor your plans for Bruce,

but I can only pray without ceasing and ask for healing on this earth—even if for a while Lord. May you touch upon his lungs, Lord, and heal them. May he be able to wake up in due time and share his walk and his faith with others. I will never give up, Lord . . . I will never stop believing in your promises—no matter what your wishes are for him. I only want to serve you. I only want to be used by you. Please Father, spare my husband; let me bring him home; let him love others to you as long as there is breath left in either one of us.

It was definitely a painful time I now entered.

I remember missing the little things. Folding towels one night at Kyle's was comforting. Unloading the dishwasher and grocery shopping was a thrill. I longed for the days of normalcy and routine.

I missed talking to Bruce.

I was a million miles away from anything familiar, and I began to question God. I wasn't only physically far away from home and our children, but mentally and emotionally I became lost. I asked God why we needed to travel down this road and why we needed to do it this way. I didn't understand, yet I knew I wanted to hang on and be strong. It was only through God's grace that I could do that. I was weak and tired, yet I managed to continue putting one foot in front of the other—and with God's help, I trudged on.

Many times God showed His love for me. I can still see myself falling apart after devastating news a CT scan showed after Bruce was on the ventilator. A doctor, whom I had never met before, walked into the room and told me the results. They weren't good. Then she grabbed my hands and said, "I'm so sorry." In her next breath she said, "You know, don't you, that Bruce will never get off the ventilator?"

I went into the small waiting room, sat on the couch, and with my head buried in my hands, I started to cry. I so desperately wanted to talk to Bruce, and suddenly the strange realization came to me that it was probably never going to happen. Before I could even think, I looked up, and there stood my brother Dean, in the doorway to the small waiting room. He just appeared. I immediately ran into his arms and sobbed. He hadn't told me he was coming.

What a blessing he was to me that day. He drove five hours from Des Moines, Iowa, only to sit with me a couple of hours, then get in his car and drive back to home that same day. Was that a coincidence? I think not. God knew what I needed. Dean was open to God's calling, and he came to hold and comfort me when I needed him the most. There was no mistake in the timing. Not only did I feel God's presence, but I felt so loved by my big brother.

The Prognosis Declared

One afternoon as I sat in Bruce's room looking at him, I journaled:

> It has only been through God's grace, love, and sustaining that we come to this place of "critical care." We rest in the Lord and wait upon Him . . . I can't think of any better hands to be in right now—even though at times it's scary, frustrating, and sad; thus, the river of tears we cry. But I know I don't cry alone because, just as God knows every hair on our head, He catches every tear we cry.

The road has been rocky. The journey tough, but to God be all the glory for carrying me during those times I couldn't stand . . . In HIM I stand, and in HIM Bruce now rests and abides—he is awaiting God's provision and healing touch.

Bruce seemed to be stable in this "critical state." That morning, the team of doctors came into the room. Leading the way was Dr. Wendt, one of the pulmonologists. She walked up to me, looked me straight in the eyes, and said, "Things don't look very good." She continued to give me her opinion that I should think about, or "re-think," how much care Bruce should receive. "What if Bruce goes into a cardiac arrest? Maybe it is best not to resuscitate him and put him through all the pain, because it won't do any good anyway." Then she added, "Of course, that's in my medical opinion."

I thought, *What nerve!*

She continued, "You realize, don't you, that he will not get off the ventilator anyway, and he won't be going home with you. Maybe his body is saying it's time, and you should just let him die in peace instead of continuing to sustain him."

What does she know? I was so mad.

I looked her straight in the eyes and said, "I will not be changing his medical directive."

On top of everything else we were dealing with, we were now told that Bruce had Acute Respiratory Distress Syndrome (A.R.D.S.), which is basically a hardening or stiffening of the alveoli in the lung. No one who has A.R.D.S. can live. This was obviously one of the deepest, darkest valleys our family had been in yet. I called Blake and Nicole with this difficult report. It was one of the hardest things I've had to do on my own so far. In discussing this new chain of events with my children, one of my greatest prayer warriors, Nicole, had the following conversation with me.

"Mommy, we prayed for Daddy's bleeding to stop in his lungs."

"That's right, Nicole, our prayers were answered. The bleeding stopped."

"Mommy, we prayed for Daddy's fever to go away."

"That's right, Nicole, our prayers were answered. The fever is gone."

"What do I need to pray for now, Mommy?"

"Sweetie, now we pray for a miracle."

The Prayer Vigil Begins

By now, the hospital staff had given up on Bruce. Through Paul's faithful continuation of e-mail updates, a prayer vigil began. He wrote:

> This note to you is to ask you to pray and consider if you would like to be part of a prayer vigil for Bruce and his family. I will provide instructions on what we are looking for, and if it is something that you feel led to do, let me know. I realize there are other folks who are praying for Bruce and Lynn that might not have access to e-mail. If you know of any that are interested, you can have them contact me. We will be starting the time of unceasing prayer for Bruce today and will be praying through Friday, April 4th. If we are led to continue after April 4th, we will contact you to see if you are led to continue on with us.

The prayer vigil began . . .

The Trip Home to Our Children

It was Monday morning, March 31st. When I woke up that day, something was different. I knew. I knew what I needed to do. It had been twenty-seven days since I had been home. I needed to get home to my children.

I prayed all month long that the Lord would let me know if I should go home to be with them or remain in Minneapolis to be near Bruce. I knew my place was with Bruce, and my children were well provided for. But today was different. In my gut, I had such a strong feeling I needed to go home. The Lord answered my prayer, and I was so thankful.

I made arrangements with my mom to come home on Wednesday. I hadn't been to church in a month, and I really missed going. By returning home on Wednesday, I'd be able to attend the evening Lenten service. Mom went home to Long Prairie, which would also give her a much needed break. I missed my children so much and felt an incredible need to be alone with them. I was anxious and excited to see them on our own turf.

When I arrived home in St. Cloud, we had just enough time to grab a quick supper, and then the kids and I headed off to church. It felt so good to be back. I missed the worship services and all the members who had truly become my second family.

After church we returned home and got ready for bed. Bruce and I had a tradition with our kids to "pray them up" each night before they went to sleep. Tonight I really looked forward to this special time with each child. It seemed it had been forever.

Nicole, our youngest, would be first. We never made it to the usual prayers that night. Instead, one question lead to another, and before I knew it, Blake had come into Nicole's room to join us. The three of us sat in the middle of her bed, and the questions just kept coming.

"Mommy, will Daddy ever come home? Will Daddy ever get off the ventilator? What is death like? Is Daddy going to die? What will we do? Doesn't God hear our prayers?" On and on the questions came. We talked about death, Daddy hanging on for us, God calling him home, and how we can help him let go and go home to God. The three of us pledged we would always tell each other the truth and never keep things from one another. It would be the three of us from here on, and we needed to be strong and supportive to each other. We cried, hugged, and let everything out. For more than two hours we bonded in a way like never before. By the time we were finished and finally ready to say good night, we were emotionally exhausted. For the first time in a month, I was there when my children needed me most, and the timing of my trip home couldn't have been more perfect.

• Chapter 17 •

Carried in Hard Times

The Phone Call

The next morning I received a call from the hospital. Bruce took another turn for the worse, and the doctors would do their best to keep him alive until the children and I arrived.

The weather that morning was terrible. It was a mix of rain and snow, with freezing drizzle. The roads were icy, and the weather service had posted travel advisories for all over Minnesota.

Our parish nurses were at church that morning. Both were good friends of Bruce's and mine. I called Gail and Julia. Through my tears on the phone, I told Gail that I felt I should be planning a funeral. I was so scared. I asked if they would get Blake and Nicole out of school for me and bring them home. They were happy to help, and I was later told that Blake's teacher started to cry when Blake was once again pulled out of the classroom. Unfortunately, these scares for my children had become routine. Each time one happened, my children and the rest of the school wondered if this time was the last.

I called our friend Paul Froland at work. I told him about the phone call I received from the hospital and that Blake, Nicole, and I needed to get to the hospital as soon as possible. The roads were hazardous to drive on, and I knew that I shouldn't be driving in that kind of weather—especially in my emotional state. Paul had a big truck, and he was happy to drive us to the Twin Cities as soon as he wrapped up a few items at work. I told him to pack an overnight bag. He could stay over night at Kyle and John's with us. I was thankful to have Paul drive. Not only was God carrying us during these unstable times, but also Paul was now literally "carrying" us to the hospital to be with Bruce.

It was a relief to arrive back at the hospital, even though I hadn't even been gone for more than twenty-four hours. The Lord had prompted me to go home so I could prepare my children. I hadn't seen that until now. All the cards were laid out on the table, and the children could say their goodbyes and give their Daddy permission to say goodbye too. What a wondrous gift the Lord gave the three of us. We received the gift of preparation, and suddenly my role as wife shifted to the role of Mom. Bruce no longer needed me as he had the previous thirty-one days, but my children needed me more than ever.

We arrived at 4:00 P.M., and Bruce rallied enough to get into a stable state. Knowing that, we stayed the night at Kyle and John's and returned early the next morning to the hospital. The roller coaster ride continued.

The Last Day this Side of Heaven

The next day was Friday, April 4th. One of my prayers was that God would prepare me for anything, even if it was God's will to take Bruce home to heaven.

Today was the day.

The entire day I felt blue. I found myself being very quiet and withdrawn. I held my children on my lap most of the day (yes, even my 13-year-old son), and we watched and waited. We talked to Bruce. We stroked his hands and head. I looked at all the tubing surrounding him and watched the oxygen saturation numbers go continuously down as the nurses gave him injections to help take fluid off his tired body. However, no fluid drained. I watched the carbon dioxide numbers rise beyond any place they should have been. His heart was now beating irregularly.

I remember at one point Kyle came into the room, grabbed my hand, and said, "Did I say something that upset you?"

"No, Kyle, this has nothing to do with you . . . I can't explain it . . . I just feel so alone." I felt alone because I knew Bruce was being called home. No one could understand what I was feeling. He was my best friend, my soul mate, the love of my life, my other half. The astonishing thing was that even though I felt so helpless, I never lost that incredible sense of peace. That peace was the same peace that I felt on New Years day. Sometime during that afternoon, I sat alone in Bruce's room and journaled the following.

April 4th Journal entry

Today Bruce is the worst he's been since he's been in the ICU. I have a feeling his organs will start to shut down soon. His blood saturation levels are at 67% and they should be at 90% plus. Despite the numbers, my heart remains calm and at peace. It's harder to see the kids watch their Daddy than it is for me. I love Bruce so much, and I pray for God to hold Bruce—just like on the wings of eagles. I pray he's not in pain. That he's in a good place. That he's worshipping God at the altar he's built in his head.

Now he's at 64% oxygen, and the machine is alarming—again. Last night Paul Froland drove

Blake, Nicole, and me to the hospital because the roads were bad. Bruce was in crisis, and his doctor called me in St. Cloud, telling me to come back immediately. They would do their best to keep Bruce alive long enough for the kids and me to get there to say goodbye.

As I look at Bruce, his hands are so swollen and bruised. He has started to bleed from his nose, and it's pooling in his mouth. Sometimes if he's not suctioned, it runs down his mouth. That bothers me.

I know there's no reverse now. His kidneys are shutting down. I watch his heart rates show irregularities now. I can tell that his heart is starting to give up too. He's fought so hard— he fought for the kids and me.

Thanks for fighting Bruce . . . it's time to stop now . . . it's time to go home. It's okay now. God is calling you. The kids and I will be okay. I feel so alone today. There are people all around me, but no one can comfort me. I need to walk through this. I need to be strong for the kids.

My journaling ended when the kids returned to the room after Aunt Kyle and Uncle John treated them to ice cream in the hospital cafeteria. I was thankful for the momentary distraction for my children. Immediately, the mood in the room became extremely somber. Tears flowed. Blake and Nicole took turns sitting on my lap. Our tears flowed throughout the afternoon and into the evening hours.

At 7 P.M. we decided we'd better get to the cafeteria before it closed for the evening. Even though I wasn't hungry, I knew the kids needed to eat. Besides, they could use another diversion. After staring mindlessly at my food, I pushed my tray aside and told everyone I wanted to head back to the room. Kyle, John, Blake, and Nicole decided to join me. I had an unsettled feeling deep within me. Once we returned to the room I could see that Bruce wasn't doing well. His blood pressure was dropping.

I held Nicole on my lap. Alarms kept going off on the machines surrounding Bruce. "Mommy, what's wrong? Why do all the machine alarms keep going off?"

"Honey, they're going off because Daddy's blood pressure keeps dropping to unsafe levels."

"Why Mommy?"

"Because Daddy is dying, Nicole."

Nicole was trying to be so brave, but through her tears she looked at me with pain in her eyes and said, "Mommy, don't say that. He's not dying. How do you know that, Mommy? That's mean to say."

I just held her and Blake and told them I was sorry.

Blake told his Daddy that he loved him and that we'd be fine. He said, "Daddy, It's okay to go."

Nicole told her Daddy that she loved him so much and that she'd always be his little "Buttercup."

We each took turns saying goodbye to Bruce. We needed him to know we'd be okay and he had permission to stop fighting and to let go.

The Entry into Heaven

At about 9:30 P.M., I asked the doctor to come out in the hallway. I had a few questions for her. I knew it was time, and I wanted to know the easiest way to medically let Bruce go. I didn't want him resuscitated and knew it was no longer necessary for the doctor to give him medication that made him stay alive unnaturally. I needed her to explain everything. I needed to know what I could expect for the children's sake, as well as my own. Will it go fast or slow? Will Bruce be in pain? I didn't want him to be in pain.

Sensing the time was near, I asked all to gather around Bruce and hold hands. I held his right hand. Kyle held his left. Then I began to pray. Through tears and a trembling voice, I thanked God for giving me the best husband a girl could ask for and for him being the best Daddy to Blake and Nicole. I asked that God now carry Bruce to Him and assure him that he had our blessings to go home to heaven.

Kyle prayed, and then in unison, we said the Lord's Prayer. She read Psalm 23 and a few other favorite Scripture verses. Once in awhile I'd look back at the heart monitor and watched as Bruce's heart rate grew slower and slower. His heartbeats were farther and farther apart, until it was a flat line except for a few insignificant blips.

At 10:00 p.m. on April 4th, Bruce died. I took the kids out of the room so the attending physicians could turn off and remove the respirator. Bruce was gone. I didn't see any reason the kids or I needed to see that. Kyle and John stayed with him. I was glad for that. Kyle said she held Bruce's hand, but she turned her head when they extracted the respirator from him. After they extracted the respirator, she turned her head back toward him. What she felt at that moment, she'll never forget. She said she actually felt his spirit leave the room. "It was incredible," she said.

Kyle and John then came to the waiting room where the kids and I were. Then we were ushered back into the room to spend some time with Bruce.

I'll never forget walking back into the ICU room. I looked at Bruce without the respirator, and I had the eeriest feeling. When I left the room just minutes earlier, my husband was lying in the hospital bed; when I came back, it was just a body I saw, not my husband. I remember the kids were glad to see the respirator off their Daddy. Nicole even commented that Daddy seemed to have a smile on his face. The nurse asked me if I wanted more time alone with Bruce.

"No," I said, "I've already said my goodbyes."

Kyle and John took down the cards and packed up his stuff. I was so glad, because I just needed to get out of the room with his body lying there. It just didn't seem right without his spirit inside. In a way, we were all relieved it was over and we were able to "pray Bruce home." I was so thankful for that.

The Dream Unveiled

After we called our family and friends to tell them that Bruce had died, we left the hospital for the last time. It was almost midnight when we left for Kyle and John's home—a place that had become my second home. My mind reeled on the drive to Kyle's. Thoughts ran through my mind. *Did what just happen, really happen? Was I really without my husband for good now?*

The roads were slushy and wet. In a funny way they depicted how my heart felt. I could tell it had snowed during the time Bruce died. I was exhausted, yet wide awake. On the side streets the snow was more evident. We turned into the area where Kyle and John lived, and soon we were about to turn into their driveway.

Suddenly, it hit me like a ton of bricks. I had seen this before. It was de ja vu. I remembered the New Years dream. It was the snow. The snow on the driveway had not melted yet. It was a total covering of perfect white, and the moonlight softly reflected off it, giving calming warmth. There were no flaws. No imperfections. It was identical to the white covering I had dreamed of on that beautiful New Years night that covered Bruce and me.

Ahh, a place of gentle peace. I knew the white snow represented the perfect healing that only God can give. On that snowy night of April 4th, God had totally and completely healed Bruce. He no longer suffered; he no longer had to fight. The Lord made everything new and flawless in Bruce's tired, worn out body. He was covered in all the purity that Christ's love and grace abundantly could give him.

Another "ah-ha" moment came to me instantly. I finally realized what the coiled tubes were that lay over Bruce in the other half of that unforgettable dream. They represented the ventilator tubes that lay over the sheets of his body for several weeks before his death. Just like in the dream, he was asleep, and he never knew what they eventually came to represent. It was the last and final step in his journey home to heaven. I now understood: God had been preparing me all along.

Thankfully, the same peace I had the night of the dream now enveloped me. Just like the perfect white snow, Bruce was healed—completely.

Christ's perfect healing blanketed Bruce.

Christ's perfect peace blanketed me.

• Chapter 18 •

A New Birthday

The Drive Home

It was well after 1:00 A.M. before we went to bed the night Bruce died, and before I knew it, the sun peered through the blinds. A new life awaited us. The idea of getting out of bed to face reality was overwhelming; there was so much to do. But where should I start? So many plans needed to be made, so many preparations arranged. From the moment I woke up after Bruce's death, I was on my own. Planning my husband's funeral was not something I wanted to do. I called Pastor Paul; he would know where to start. I was told as soon as I got back to St. Cloud to go home, pick out clothes for Bruce, and then go to the funeral home to make preparations. Pastor Paul would meet us there.

Once in the car, questions awaited me. "Mom, you're not going to have to go back to work again, are you? We don't want you to go back to work. Please!" Then came one that surprised me. "Mom, you're not going to get married again, are you?"

"Where did that come from?" I responded.

Apparently, Blake and Nicole had already had this conversation. I took a deep breath and shot up an arrow prayer.

"Thanks for being honest with me guys on what you're thinking and the questions you have. You need to know that I will always be honest with you and up front. To answer your first question, I will try my best *not* to go back to work right away. I need to let things settle down, and then you'll be the first to know what the game plan is. But for now, please don't worry about it, okay?

"Now, as for your second question, Mommy doesn't profess to know the mind of God, so I honestly can not say I'd never get married again. I don't know the plans God has for me or for any of us at this point. However, I can assure you that getting married again is the farthest thing from my mind right now. It will be some time before I can even think about that possibility. You two are my main priority. I will do everything in my power to be the best Mom, playing double duty to you in Daddy's absence. For now, you are safely stuck with just *me*."

When we returned home, the first thing that caught my eye was Bruce's recliner in the living room. My eyes seemed to be transfixed on it, because it was covered completely with BoTie's black cat hair. She loved Bruce. Mom said BoTie curled up in his chair all the time, especially at night. I'm convinced BoTie knew Bruce was sick all along; probably even before the rest of us.

Snapping out of my trance, I wasted no time and scurried up to our bedroom. While standing in front of our closet staring at Bruce's suits, the telephone rang. It was my friend Laurie.

"Lynn, I'm so sorry . . . how are you doing?" Her voice cracked, and I could tell she was crying.

"How do you pick something out for your husband to wear in a casket?" I painfully choked out.

"I'll be right there," and the phone went dead.

Within minutes, Laurie was comforting me in my bedroom, holding me as we shared a river of tears.

"Now, let's pick out something nice for Bruce to wear," she said emphatically.

Laurie was a blessing at the very time I needed a friend. Again, I couldn't help but think about God and His timing.

Within half an hour, my friend Julia and my mom arrived. Feeling Mom's arms wrapped around me in a loving, secure embrace was just the medicine I needed. I reverted to being a little girl again. I hoped that her hug would make my world better and my hurt go away. She held me like she never wanted to let go. I didn't want her to either. Softly she whispered in my ear, "I'm so sorry. It's okay to cry honey. I understand." She did understand. She had lost my dad to cancer several years earlier.

Thank you God for Mothers.

Kyle soon arrived, and Blake, Kyle, and I headed to the funeral home. We had to make arrangements. After spending hours at the funeral home making decisions I never dreamed I'd make at such a young age, I came home to a house full of people. Someone had brought pizzas, and I remember sitting at the kitchen table, knowing I should eat, but all I could do was cry. As I looked down at the pizza in front of me, tormenting thoughts filled my mind. I hunkered down in my own little world.

I just picked out Bruce's casket, bought a cemetery plot, picked out clothes he'll be buried in, chose the service folder, and much more still needs to be planned for the funeral service. This isn't right. This shouldn't be happening.

It had only been twenty-four hours. The next two days were filled with more funeral arrangements—choosing songs, Scripture readings, and who would speak at Bruce's funeral. There was one song that Bruce told me he wanted for his funeral someday, but I couldn't remember the name of it. I knew a few lines of the song, but that was it. People were searching the Internet for me, calling radio stations, searching through their own CD collections, but the song never surfaced. I felt so bad.

The Newspaper Tribute

It was time for the viewing at the funeral home. A steady stream of people came. I was so moved when all the Boy Scouts came together in uniform to pay their respects. Our son, Blake, was touched, because they were his peers—his Boy Scout troop. Bruce's oncologist came to see her "Brucie" and to say goodbye, as did several others from Parker Hughes Cancer Treatment Center. An abundance of flowers and plants filled the funeral home. With many well wishes and wonderful stories of Bruce, I felt my heart overflowing with love.

At close to 9:00 P.M., things seemed to be winding down, and I noticed one lone man going up to pay his respects to Bruce. I had never seen him before. After some time alone at the casket, he came up to me, grabbed my hands, and introduced himself.

"You must be Lynn. My name is Dick Andzenge. I knew Bruce from St. Cloud State University where I am a professor. I also knew Bruce through *Men of Faith* and heard about him when I became involved in the Boy Scouts. I write for the St. Cloud Times newspaper and would like your permission to publish a tribute to Bruce in tomorrow's St. Cloud Times morning edition. I couldn't get here earlier because I needed to finish writing the article to get it submitted to the editor. It is awaiting publication upon your approval."

Without hesitation, I gave my blessing. Bruce knew a lot of people, but I had yet to discover just how significantly he had affected others. The following is what Dick sent via e-mail and what appeared the next morning in our local newspaper:

Lynn:

I wish to say again that I am really sorry that you and the kids will have to move on without the physical presence of Bruce. However, I am sure you know Bruce is safe with the Lord, and God used him during his short life to touch many lives. No one can comfort you or get you to understand the mystery of His grace but God Himself. Your husband was a very special person, and I trust that He who took him from you will take care of you and the children. This is the article I am submitting to St. Cloud Times in memory of Bruce.

HIS SHORT LIFE MADE A BIG DIFFERENCE
By: Dick Andzenge

Someone suggested recently that Jesus was not even forty when He died, yet for such a short life, He impacted the world more than any human before and after Him. We all long for a long life and grieve deeply when we lose loved ones, even though we know that all who live shall also die. The grief becomes even more intense when a life is lost at a relatively young age. For relatives and friends of those who pass away at an early age, only time can heal the pain that results from the loss. The truth is that the quality of life has little to do with how long we live, rather, on what we do with the life we have while we are alive.

Like many people in St. Cloud, I read of the death of Bruce MacKenzie in the St. Cloud Times and was moved to tears. As I read the obituary and thought about the Bruce that I knew, it occurred to me that Bruce had done in a short life span more than a fair share of service to humanity and to the community. His life, though short, touched and enriched many lives, including mine, and needs to be celebrated.

Since he graduated from St. Cloud State University in 1985, Bruce has been an inspiration to everyone whose life he touched. From 1985 to 1990, he served as District Executive Director and Senior Executive with the Boy Scouts of America, Central Minnesota Council. I was not in St. Cloud at the time and not associated with the Boy Scouts, but since I was asked to join the Boy Scouts board recently, almost everybody associated with the group has shared the wonderful contributions Bruce made to the Scouts during those years.

I did not know Bruce until a friend introduced me to the Men of Faith Ministry, where I met Bruce who was a Co-Chair of the group. Although we were from different backgrounds, Bruce and I connected immediately as people who had far more in common than we had that was different. We both had a passion for our faith, the St. Cloud Community, and St. Cloud State University. Bruce was deeply committed to a life of genuine kindness and friendship with everyone he met. He touched many lives by simply listening and sharing his assuring smile and stubborn confidence that all is well. In many ways, Bruce represented the best that St. Cloud has to offer. Bruce was always a friend upon whom you knew you could depend. It seemed as though Bruce was everybody's friend. His life, though short, was a beautiful testimony of the best we could be to one another.

Death at a young age seems cruel as it leaves a young widow with children confused, scared, and even angry about the apparent injustice of denying them the beautiful completeness of a loving husband and father. While there are no words of comfort that can erase the pain, we can hope that the memories of a well-lived life will endure. Many people in the community who did not know Bruce cannot appreciate that he was a special gift to the community, but those who knew him and were touched by him must remember what Bruce would say, "The ministry goes on!"

During his last few years, Bruce was the Executive Director of Development at the SCSU Foundation. For a secular institution that struggles with conflict and indifference, Bruce had a refreshing passion and gentleness, and a commitment to the institution that he loved. I hope that at the university also, his memories will endure as an example of the best that the institution produces.

It is my hope that Bruce's widow, Lynn, and their children will reap the fruits of the love and compassion that Bruce planted.

What a beautiful tribute Dick gave to Bruce and a treasured legacy he left to our children, the community at large, and me through his article. His words will forever remain a blessing in our lives. I thank God for Dick and his sharing with me and others a part of Bruce I would have never known had it not been for his accolade.

The Funeral

A beautiful spring day greeted me the morning of the funeral. It was now time to wake the children and get ready. The funeral was planned. I knew who would sing, who would speak, Bruce's favorite Scripture verses that would be read, yet something was missing. Was I to speak? I was unsure.

As I took my shower that morning, I cried out to God once again. *God if you want me to speak, you need to tell me.* My tears washed down the drain with the soap as I finished my shower. With my robe on and towel wrapped around my head, I walked upstairs. Before I realized it, I sat at the computer, and my fingers just flew. I printed out what I had typed, got ready, and began the drive to church.

Categorizing my thoughts as I drove, I recalled the two days before Bruce died. The weather was incredibly harsh—ice storms, sleet, rain, wind, and even snow. Today was different. It was a beautiful spring, April day. If I didn't know better, I would have thought the seasons jumped from winter to the heart of spring within the past forty-eight hours. A blue, cloudless sky embraced us on this special morning. My children and I began calling April 4th "Daddy's New Birthday Celebration." It was as if this day, April 8th, was just the birthday party.

Those arriving at church left their coats in their cars. The sunshine penetrated my very core and warmed me like a big, warm, fleece blanket. Inhaling the fresh breeze was refreshing and invigorating, and there was a fragrance of new life that filtered through the air. All the matted debris that lay on the ground from winter seemed to melt away. I felt such peace.

Once at church, I was directed to drive my car directly behind the hearse parked in front of the church. Again, life seemed surreal. After parking my car, I went to the church office. I wanted to talk to Pastor Paul about the words I typed that morning and ask him if I should speak at Bruce's funeral. Without hesitation, he suggested I have someone else read it. From past experience, he said I may be too emotional. I reluctantly agreed and asked Dan Bates to read it. He could do so after he gave his comments about Bruce and Prince of Peace Lutheran School.

Music flooded our church and all our praise choirs joined forces. The choir from the school even sang. School was cancelled for the day so that all the teachers, students, and families could attend the funeral. Many came to know and love Bruce and our family, and we all united together in suffering and celebration.

Before the casket was closed and the service began, I took Blake and Nicole's hands; together we went to say our last goodbyes. It was hard, yet the music that filled the air continued to point me to a higher place, a higher purpose. None of this was fair; yet even though I could not see the reasons for this injustice, I knew I needed, to be strong for my children. I needed to endure, because this was the road the Lord had chosen for us at this time in our lives. I didn't need to understand the "whys" right now, but rather, to believe that God led us down this road for a reason. We would need to rely on Him to walk with us on this uncharted journey. Better yet, we needed to believe He would carry us through that day and every day after.

Chapter 19

The Ministry Goes On

The Service Begins

Praise music permeated throughout the funeral service. Near the beginning of the service, Carol Copeland, one of the praise leaders that Bruce and I often lead worship services with said the following as soft music accompanied her words:

> Bruce has been a big part of every music ministry here at Trinity. As a worship leader, he encouraged the congregation to worship: that is, to ascribe worth, honor, and praise to our Holy Lord. He challenged us to move past our mere humanness and truly experience a complete and total offering of ourselves in worship. Bruce is no longer hindered by human frailties but is singing praises to the Lord unceasingly. What deep and lasting comfort there is in knowing that God inhabits the praises of His people and that we are forever connected to Bruce and all the saints of all time as we fall on our knees in worship.

After Carol's comments, several spoke to eulogize Bruce, then Pastor Paul ended with a beautiful message. The neat thing about those who spoke at the funeral was that everyone had one main theme in their comments, and I found it remarkably similar to Bruce's cry the day he found out he had cancer. I have taken a few excerpts from their comments that seemed to tie Bruce's life together and encapsulated the "valley walk" we traveled.

The Prince of Peace Passion
Message from Dan Bates

The first person to eulogize Bruce was Dan Bates. Bruce and Dan had worked together for years on the Prince of Peace Lutheran School board. Both had served as president of the school board and dedicated their lives to see to the completion of the school. Dan's comments were as follows:

> I met Lynn in 1995, when I started working for Manpower. I met Bruce for the first time while my wife, Cheri, and I were still living in the Twin Cities. We would come to Trinity every once in a while for church with Cheri's parents. I really got to know Bruce several years later after my wife and I moved to Sauk Rapids and became full-time members at Trinity Lutheran Church. I had no idea when I first met them what an impact they would have on my life and the life of my family.
>
> In 1998, Bruce and I were at a board retreat for the St. Cloud Area Chamber of Commerce, and he talked to me on a break about this "thing"—this "initiative" he was trying to get

off the ground. The idea was to create a new, community-wide school, growing out of the 115-year tradition of Trinity. Well, he didn't have to talk to me long to get me on board, and I stayed for the long haul. I'm sure there are many of you here today that have a very similar story. Bruce had an amazing way of instilling his enthusiasm in others. That's a trait I came to love and respect in him and hope to learn someday. Anyway, I know you've all heard about Prince of Peace, because it was Bruce's vision—his passion—and all you had to do was ask him about it, and he'd be off. In fact, if you let him, he probably wouldn't stop talking for quite a while.

For the past year, Bruce hasn't been able to be at our meetings, physically anyway. He has definitely been there in spirit. Our board continually returns to Bruce's ideas, thoughts, and his vision for Prince of Peace. We've met with him at his home, had countless phone calls, and countless e-mails. Bruce is the catalyst that brought us all together, brought this whole thing together, and brought us to the point we are at today—three preschool campuses across St. Cloud and as of July 1st, finally operating Prince of Peace Lutheran School. Bruce had an amazing way of getting hundreds of people together, working in a cohesive group, to make the vision of Prince of Peace a reality. In fact, Bruce pointed out that this initiative may have been the first time in over a hundred years that multiple congregations in Central Minnesota have come together to make a major impact as one Lutheran Church body; an amazing feat to say the least.

Bruce always said, "God gave us this vision, and we are the people on earth who will fulfill this vision—this 'God Inspired Vision.'" He taught us all to see Prince of Peace and Trinity as more than the amazing Lutheran School that has taught thousands of children to more deeply know the Gospel of Jesus Christ over the past 115 years. As our mission statement says, Prince of Peace is a "lifetime educational ministry for children and families based on the Gospel of Jesus Christ, focusing on academic excellence and service to our community."

Bruce always impressed me with his dedication to church and his tremendous faith, his commitment to his family and friends, and his incredible drive to do the best in everything he did. Wherever you went, you saw Bruce—a business event in the community, a SCSU Husky's Hockey game, a worship service at church, an event at Trinity school—he was there and was usually involved in some capacity. His faith, his drive, and his commitment to others touched whoever knew him. As part of Bruce's Prayer Warrior updates that Lynn and Paul have been sharing, my wife and I forwarded the e-mails to our own group of friends and family on our Prayer Warrior's list. Even people that have never met Bruce, people from all over the country, commented on what a strong and true faith he had—and it never wavered, throughout the entire process.

Even when Bruce was "deep in the valley of chemo" he sent this e-mail to me one afternoon in June, eleven days before his birthday, a birthday we share.

Dan: Here's the final, approved version of the by-laws. Sorry it took me so long. You know, for a guy who's not working, loafing around in a chair most of the day, I sure have been slacking off. Better shape up here; you guys won't put up with this much longer.

Praise Almighty God for everyone who is working on this "call" from Him to start this ministry. One thing I'm learning, we've got to fully trust Him, His timing, and His will on all this. Instead of praying that He helps us move this along, we need to pray that His hand directs everything we do, that we fully trust Him for the provision we need (money, hands to help, etc.), and that our full desire is that we remain in His wonderful will in all we do. I've learned enormous insights about trusting Jesus. About asking Him specifically for the things I need like "please help me to be well enough tonight, Jesus, to attend my children's concert"—a prayer he answered despite how I felt when I prayed it, and about unconditionally believing that He is answering them.

Dan, might I even be so bold as to suggest that at the June meeting, you ask everyone to hold hands, and say, "Tonight we are going to God in prayer, in full trust, full acceptance, and full expectation as we offer up our needs in this ministry." God is impressing upon me that He doesn't just want Prince of Peace to arise and begin—He wants all of us to be awash with Him and His light, so that He glorifies these efforts and in turn His people will glorify Him!! From my perspective now, I simply cannot bring myself to consider things or thoughts or actions that are not in line with His will and pleasing to Him. And amazingly, I have never been so truly blessed in my entire life.

I love all of you, but Jesus loves you more.

Dan concluded, "Thank you for giving to the Lord, Bruce, I'm so glad that you gave."

The Big Win
Message from Lynn

After Dan gave his eulogy, he was supposed to read what I had typed, but emotions overcame him, and he was having trouble speaking. He told me after the service that when he walked up to the podium, he touched Bruce's casket as he walked by it. Instantly, it felt like electricity went through his body. He couldn't shake that feeling and was moved to tears.

As I sat in the front pew watching Dan try to compose himself, it was as if something or someone kept nudging my right shoulder, whispering in my ear, *Lynn, go up there. You need to help Dan out. Read what you wrote . . . you're strong enough to do it.* Before I realized it, I stood up and began walking forward. Looking up, Dan was surprised to see me approach the lectern. He hugged me and sat back down. For reasons I didn't understand, God wanted me to share the words He gave me that morning—not someone else.

Placing the page I typed that morning on the podium, I looked out at the packed church as hundreds of faces stared at me in utter disbelief that I was going to speak. My hands grabbed the sides of the podium to steady myself. Complete silence flooded the church, and I took a deep breath.

> Good afternoon. Last June, Bruce bought a book entitled *My Utmost for His Highest* by Oswald Chambers. It is a classic daily devotional book that has been read by millions of people all over the world. Since the beginning of Bruce's diagnosis of Stage IV cancer, he has read this small devotional book, along with his Bible, every day. Every day he spent time alone with God in prayer, many times in prayer for many of you. What impressed me the most about this little devotional book was what he wrote on the inside cover. It read:
>
> "Presented to: Bruce MacKenzie
>
> By: Himself!
>
> On the Occasion of: 'A Need for a Deeper Walk'
>
> Date: June '02"
>
> I was aware he purchased the book shortly after his cancer diagnosis, but I didn't know what was written on the inside cover—until this morning. Not only was "A Need for a Deeper

Walk" written inside this book, but I *know* it was written upon his heart. If Bruce were here today, he would be asking each of us about our walk with the Lord, so I'm doing it for him.

Where is your walk with the Lord at?

Bruce was a great husband and father to our two children. But it is what made him great that I will miss—he would rather serve than be served. He'd rather take risks for the Lord than melt into the crowds; he'd rather lead by God's wisdom, rather than his own; and he'd rather be obedient first, only to see the blessings later. He truly lived "walking by faith and not by sight."

The day Bruce found out that he had cancer, we went to see Pastor Paul to share this news. Pastor Paul and I were saddened, and it felt like we were punched in the stomach. But Bruce calmly looked at us and said, "Hey, I win either way. I win if I beat this thing, am healed, and live on this earth a while longer with my family and friends. And I win if the Lord calls me home to be with Him. But either way, I *win*."

Wow. What faith. Praise God, and may we all have the eyes to see the real victory during this Easter season and be able to say, regardless of what happens today, "either way, *I win*."

After a momentary pause, I picked up my notes and returned to the pew.

The Place of Surrender
Message from Paul Froland

Paul Froland was next. Bruce and Paul had grown to become such good friends. They shared their faith, began the local *Men of Faith* ministry together, and held each other accountable in whatever areas they struggled with in their lives. Paul began:

> The *Men of Faith* ministry was birthed out of our desire to serve the Lord and to serve the men in the greater St. Cloud area. "To ultimately advance the kingdom of our Lord and Savior Jesus Christ." Bruce, Cameron Schroeder, Dale Kuklok, Tony Hall, and I have seen again how the Lord has honored and blessed those desires that He placed in our hearts.
>
> April 25th, 2002, changed Bruce's life forever, and for that matter it changed the lives of everyone connected to Bruce and Lynn, certainly everyone here today, along with everyone they came in contact with in the last eleven months.
>
> Bruce was scheduled to share with the *Men of Faith* on March 15th a message that was on his heart. He was unable to do so due to his hospitalization. Unfortunately, we do not have the text to the message, but we do know that it had to do with "surrendering."
>
> There is no doubt that Bruce had committed his life to his Lord and Savior, Jesus Christ. But over the past 11 months, a process of the

molding and shaping that the Lord was doing in Bruce resulted in (complete) surrender.

A good friend of ours, Jeanie Schroeder, said this of Bruce upon his passing, "We know that Bruce just got to heaven ahead of us, much like his life here on earth, always a leader, always a go-getter, and always focused on Christ as King." I believe the Lord used Bruce as a leader, a tool, and an empty vessel to lead many of us to that place of surrender during these past eleven months.

Another good friend of mine commented just this morning that Bruce left it all out on the field. It is my prayer that we too can say the same thing—that we've left it all on the field. If there is any question in your mind whether you have surrendered your life to our Savior, Jesus Christ, I pray that you answer that before you leave today.

Once we get to that place of surrender, watch out—for that is where you will see the Lord move mightily through us as empty vessels, just as we have witnessed how the Lord moved and worked through Bruce to touch so many lives and to bring the "Good News" of salvation and the love of God to so many people.

I am reminded of some verses in Isaiah. I believe it shows us what to look for when we reach that place of surrender that we saw in our Deliverer, the Lord Jesus Christ, and what we have also witnessed in our dear brother Bruce. Isaiah 61:1–3 reads: "The Spirit of the Sovereign Lord is on me, because the Lord has anointed me to preach the good news, to the poor. He has sent me to bind up the broken-hearted, to proclaim freedom for the captives and release from darkness from the prisoners, and to proclaim the year of the Lord's favor and the day of vengeance of our God, to comfort all who mourn, and provide for those who grieve in Zion—to bestow on them a crown of beauty instead of ashes, the oil of gladness instead of mourning, and a garment of praise instead of a spirit of despair. They will be called Oaks of righteousness, a planting of the Lord for the display of his splendor."

It brings sweet comfort in knowing that Bruce's battle and life was not over until God had accomplished every last bit of good for which he could use it. I can already see that the seed of "surrender" the Lord had planted in Bruce is producing a great harvest of souls for the Kingdom.

My heart and prayers are with you, Lynn, Blake, Nicole, and the rest of the family; the Lord loves you and cares for you.

Thank you, and may the Lord bless you.

The 4 "F's"
Message from Kyle

After Dan, Paul, and I spoke, Bruce's sister, Kyle, went up to the lectern. She spoke of the four "F's" from Bruce's life—Faith, Family, Friends, and Fun. Through many funny stories and anecdotes, Kyle had the attention of all present. Laughter erupted often, and she brought out the side of Bruce that was always goofing around, making others laugh. She ended her message relating how the four "F's" were directly lived out during Bruce's cancer journey. Her final comments spoke volumes about how Bruce lived them out, even in the face of death. Pausing momentarily to scan the faces of those in attendance, poised and confident, Kyle continued:

> With every decision Bruce made, he made it after prayer. Doctors and nurses knew we were praying for them.

A pregnant pause followed each of Kyle's comments.

> Bruce said, "God Bless You," when someone finished sticking him or completed yet another test. Someone would come to take him for a procedure, and he'd say, "Wait! Listen to this!" and proceed to read Scripture that he was pondering. He referred to the 23rd Psalm when he would talk about "Yea though I walk through the valley of the shadow of chemo."

> Bruce was always positive, even in the face of tough news and tough treatment. We had a symbolic mascot, which was a small frog

beanie. His name was simply Frog. Frog, who had become our mascot, stood for *Fully Rely On God*. He went to all chemo appointments, procedures, and was with Bruce in ICU. Frog even rested on Bruce's chest as he passed into eternity.

Prayer was central. Some would say our biggest prayer wasn't answered. But God did answer; it just wasn't what we hoped. We talked about how it would be easy if our God was a God who never heals. Or if our God was a God who always heals. But our God is a God who sometimes heals in the way we would hope. However, despite God's final answer (in Bruce's life), we've had abundant blessings and answers to prayers.

Bruce, despite cancer, was always getting on with God's business. He would want the same for us. We all must take time to grieve appropriately, but then to get back to God's business—to do what God is calling each of us to do for Him.

To . . . carry on!

The Seed
Message from Pastor Paul

Pastor Paul gave the final message at Bruce's funeral. His text came from John 12:23–28, and the theme for his message was "Father, Glorify Your Name." He scanned his surroundings. People crammed into every church pew available and filled every extra chair. A video camera was set up in the balcony. The service was filmed and broadcast to those seated in the church basement. The camera focused in on Pastor Paul. He began:

> Grace and Peace in Christ Jesus to all of you this day; you for whom Bruce was a beloved son, brother, uncle, husband, father; a good friend, colleague, neighbor; trusted Promise Keeper, Man of Faith, Iron Man; gifted churchman, evangelist, leader/visionary, student/teacher of Scripture, disciple of Christ, and brother in Christ.
>
> Despite the victory over death we celebrate here, today is a sad day. It is Lent after all, a time we relive the suffering and death of our Lord Jesus. The suffering and death of Bruce is also on our minds. Jesus and Bruce: they have much in common. That was on my mind as I considered the Gospel lesson from last Sunday (John 12:23–28).
>
> It's easy to eulogize or say a good word about Bruce, as is being done here today. But I'm going to take that a step further and, without being too presumptuous and canonize Bruce, I'm going to compare Bruce to Jesus. They both died young, deprived of life, with so much potential for good.
>
> It was exactly one month before he died that Bruce entered the hospital, on the day before Ash Wednesday. This last month was his Lenten journey, a time of suffering that ended on a dark,

dreary Friday. In fact, Thursday and Friday of last week were two of the most miserable days of the winter. 10:00 P.M. last Friday night was Bruce's "hour." And his death, like that of Jesus, brought glory to the Father's name.

"Tragic" is the word we might use to describe the death of both Bruce and Jesus. Tragic because their deaths appear so senseless and unfair. The "why" question keeps coming up.

The answer for Jesus, of course, can be found in two phrases: "the hour" and "the seed." "The hour has come," Jesus says. The hour: it's a phrase that looms throughout John's Gospel and on occasion, rings like a muffled bell announcing something. Early on at the wedding in Cana, Jesus told His mother that His "hour had not yet come." Several times, the Jews tried to arrest Him but couldn't, the reason being His "hour had not yet come." But here, for the first time, Jesus says, "The hour has come." The final bell is tolling.

Later, with His disciples in the upper room, John writes that, "Jesus knew the time had come for him to leave this world and go to the Father." And in His prayer that evening, He begins, "Father, the time has come." The Father set the clock; it was the right time.

The hour had come for a kernel of wheat to fall to the ground and die so that it could produce many seeds. A seed has to die in order to fulfill its purpose. Death brings life—in the form of many seeds! That was Jesus' mission. What could He say, "Father, save me from this hour?" No. "It was for this very reason I came to this hour. Father, glorify Your name!" Indeed, the Father's glory shines most brightly in the forgiveness won by Jesus' death. The hour of His death would be God's most shining moment.

Jesus' death—tragic, yet necessary!

There are, no doubt, those today who would look up here a bit outraged and be thinking, "Tragic, yes; but certainly not necessary." Bruce, today, I believe would say, "It was for this very reason I came to this hour. Father, glorify your name!" I don't know why this was necessary. But I have a hunch it might have something to do with "the seed." Two thoughts come to mind here. First of all, the lesson of the seed reminds us that we need to die before we can live. That was a characteristic of Bruce. Most of his life, he was dying to live. He knew what St. Paul meant: "I have been crucified with Christ, and it is no longer I who live but Christ lives in me." Or as Jesus puts it here, "The man who loves his life will lose it, while the man who hates his life in this world (i.e. dies to the world) will keep it for eternal life."

By our baptism, we were buried with Christ in His death. Remembering our baptism, and the daily repenting and trusting in forgiveness that remembering brings, causes us to die to sin and rise to a new life; the life where "Christ lives in me." Death opens the door to fullness of life, not just beyond the grave, but already here, and now.

Secondly, "if a seed dies, it produces many seeds." There are very few people I know who have influenced others the way Bruce has in his brief life. Let me simply say . . . I believe we have yet to see the fullness of God's glory demonstrated through the life—and especially now the death—of His beloved son Bruce. "Many seeds!" God is working powerfully through him. "Father, glorify Your name!"

Jesus and Bruce: their deaths were "tragic, yet necessary." That's also what made them at the same time "sad, yet joyful." That's the schizophrenia of Good Friday.

We sing the sad songs of Lent. Many choose to fast, give something up, or show restraint in their lives in some other way. But these expressions of grief are always conditioned by the "Father, glorify Your name" of Easter.

Death leads to resurrection for Jesus; victory, forgiveness, and life. Lent is a roller coaster that ends in an "Alleluia, Christ is risen! and the joyful praise of Easter." That's what makes Friday "Good."

Speaking of a roller coaster, how about this last year! In Sunday's Epistle lesson from Hebrews we're told, "During the days of Jesus' life on earth, he offered up prayers and petitions with loud cries and tears to the one who could save him from death." A few prayers were said, a few tears shed for Bruce, too. On numerous occasions, he was in "the valley."

But there were also the mountain tops. Just two days before he went into the hospital for the last time, he sang with the worship team up here. It was "Transfiguration Sunday," and it was a mountain top experience. Think of it: he gave some of his last good breaths to praise God before he descended into his Lenten journey. You know that Transfiguration Sunday and Easter Sunday frame Lent. Bruce never did get to celebrate another Easter here on earth after his diagnosis. Maybe in a microcosm, his last year is a reminder of the time we all live between the Easters. We celebrate Jesus' resurrection, and we anticipate our own. We go through our valleys and ride our roller coasters, until finally the end comes, and we join the saints in heaven and those left on earth in that final and unending "Alleluia." That's what makes last Friday "good"!

I'm going to miss Bruce. I'm going to miss his positive nature, his smile, his sense of humor, his concern for others, and his respect for the sacred. The first time I met him was the day I was installed as pastor here nearly eight years ago. Before the installation service, he and Lyn Recknor were up here in the sacristy. They were in the hand bell choir, which was playing for the service—the only two men bold enough to be in the bell choir. They were wearing their little bow ties and laughing about something, which they were often prone to do. And as we introduced each other, Bruce did his little genuflect (bend the knee in reverence), something he would do many times after that. I realized he wasn't doing this sarcastically or mockingly, even though he would smile when he did it. Nor was he reverencing me, per se. He was showing respect for my office and the One whom I, as pastor, represent. Bowing before his pastor, being in a bell choir, singing with a worship team . . . Bruce was a "Real Man."

Today is a reminder for us that the shortness of life gives urgency to reaching our goals before human powers fail us; or, as the collect puts it, "to work while it is day, before the night comes when no one can work." Bruce's greatest goal, his passion these last years, was the task he took on to create a Lutheran School Association and to build Prince of Peace Lutheran School. That was his vision and final kingdom goal in life. He poured his life into it.

I recall an analogy Bruce would often make from his bell choir days. He'd say that in order for a song to be played, every bell needs to do its part. It may be small, but if it's missing, the song will suffer.

In the song that was Bruce's vision, an important bell has been silenced. May I be so bold as to issue a challenge: that we join together in concert to build Prince of Peace Lutheran School Association as a legacy to Bruce. But more so—and (I'm sure that) Bruce would concur—to do it because the hour has come, the seed has died, and it's time to produce many seeds.

So, "Father, glorify Your name!" Amen.

The service came to a close.

Chapter 20

His Purpose Unfolds

The Second Puzzle Piece

Flash forward . . .

I held the unassuming puzzle piece that Pastor Craig Moore gave me. We were finally cleared to proceed to the cemetery. After a short service, we returned to the school gymnasium for cake and ice cream. Being surrounded by the presence of God and the love of others sustained and carried us throughout that indescribable day.

When we returned home, exhaustion penetrated every part of my being. Family members stayed for a few days, but one by one they left. Life resumed to an odd normalcy. The kids returned to school. I discovered everything that once was normal now seemed foreign—again. I had just spent the last several days submerged in funeral arrangements; thirty-two days at a hospital sixty miles from home; and ten months before that, dealing with the challenges cancer brings.

Cancer, that uninvited intruder, somehow burst right into our home and changed our family's life. I needed to learn how to live again. Bruce was gone, and nothing would ever be the same. In a strange way, I needed to discover a "new normal."

As days passed, I crawled back into bed after dropping Blake and Nicole off at school. I was physically, emotionally, and spiritually fatigued. I needed rest.

One week after the funeral, I continued with my new routine. I had just fallen back to sleep when I was awakened by the telephone ringing. Startled, I grabbed the phone in the bedroom and said, "MacKenzie's." A women's voice answered.

"Hi, Lynn, I bet you don't know who this is."

Before I could even respond, she continued, "This is Sandy." *She sounded so excited.*

I was surprised to hear her voice. Sandy was a business acquaintance from the days I managed a local temporary service. I always liked Sandy and connected with her as if we had been lifelong friends. I was glad to hear from her; yet I was curious about why she called. We hadn't spoken in years.

"Lynn, you don't know this, but I was at Bruce's funeral. Someone had been forwarding the e-mails about him, and I was following his progress. When I heard he died, I was so sad and felt drawn to attend the funeral. I was doing fine throughout most of the funeral, until you got up and spoke. You recapped what Bruce told Pastor Paul in his office the afternoon you found out about his cancer. You told us of how Bruce said he 'won either way'—remember?"

"Of course I remember," I replied. *I wasn't sure where she was going with this.*

"Well, I was sitting in the back of the church. After you shared, I suddenly got a pit in my stomach. I realized I couldn't say that. You know . . . that I won either way. I went home, blew the dust off my Bible, and began searching. Searching for what, I wasn't sure, but I still searched. I knew there was something missing. For days I couldn't get Bruce's funeral out of my mind. Somehow it changed me, but I didn't know how. Today I made a phone call to Jim Stigman regarding business matters. I don't think we even got to the business part of my phone call, because we started to talk about Bruce's funeral."

"I told Jim about the part where you spoke and Bruce had just announced that he won either way. I realized that I couldn't say that. I even told Jim how I blew the dust off my Bible and searched for something, but I wasn't sure what. At about that time, Jim interrupted me and asked if I had ever asked Jesus Christ into my life as my personal Lord and Savior. I said, 'No.'

"'Sandy, would you like to?' Jim asked.

"'Yes!' I replied. At that moment, Jim prayed with me. I asked Jesus into my heart. I felt a ton of bricks fall from my shoulders. Ever since I prayed with Jim, I've been happy, feeling free. I'm walking on cloud nine! I found what I was searching for. Jim told me I should tell at least two other people. He asked that I call you."

Elated, I told Sandy I was incredibly happy for her and thanked her over and over for sharing her story with me. Bruce would do anything to share the free gift of salvation. He lived his faith boldly. I told Sandy that if Bruce knew his cancer and now his death would save even one other person, Bruce would have been standing at the front of the line saying, "Pick me, God, pick me."

For some strange reason, I found myself sharing with Sandy the story of the puzzle piece given to me after Bruce's funeral. Suddenly, another "Ah-ha" moment hit me. I realized I had just been given a second piece to the puzzle. Sandy! I started to understand what God was trying to show me through Bruce's suffering and now death. That's just like God to speak in unconventional ways—a simple puzzle piece.

Through Bruce's death, Sandy had come to know life-eternal life. It reminded me of a Bible passage when Jesus was talking about going after one lost sheep until it is found. In Luke 15:5–7, He says, "And when he finds it, he joyfully puts it on his shoulders and goes home. Then he calls his friends and neighbors together and says, 'Rejoice with me; I have found my lost sheep.' I tell you that in the same way there will be more rejoicing in heaven over one sinner who repents than over ninety-nine righteous persons who do not need to repent."

Bruce was now rejoicing in heaven over Sandy. I couldn't think of anything greater to come from losing my husband than to know that his life and now his death had somehow influenced the salvation of others. In life, and even death, there is, and will always be—hope.

Bruce took nothing physically with him. His body wasted away. The only thing that mattered was his faith in the Lord and Savior. There was no accident that Sandy received those e-mails and felt compelled to attend the funeral. It appeared like the last puzzle piece for Bruce fit one that was yet to be found. Through his witness, in life and death, Sandy found God. That was the second puzzle piece.

After our conversation ended, I pondered about life. We are not given all the pieces at once. Often it's one at a time, but it's always just at the right time. Eventually we see how our lives fit into God's bigger puzzle. I am reminded of 1 Corinthians 13:12, which says, "Now we see but a poor reflection as in a mirror; then we shall see face to face. Now I know in part; then I shall know fully, even as I am fully known." In a parallel way, we only know our life's puzzle as we look back in hindsight and see how the pieces of our past fit together. When we look ahead, we only see the parts that are missing, the pieces that God has yet to give us.

Romans 8:28 says, "And we know that in all things God works for the good of those who love him, who have been called according to his purpose." Who are we to question God's ultimate plan, I may have wondered—now I believe.

The E-mail from a Good Friend

Sundays were hard. Worship had always been so special to Bruce and me. Now I sat alone. During the sermons, Bruce always held my hand, and often when we stood, he'd gently place his hand on my back. I miss his touch.

I remember one Sunday, shortly after Bruce's funeral, being especially difficult. I don't know if it was the words to a song, something said during the prayers, the sermon, or going up to communion alone. But my tears wouldn't stop. After I returned to the pew, I put my head in my lap. I covered my face and wept. Of all times, I had to be next to the aisle. Mentally, I shut myself out from the rest of the world—I had to. Startled, I felt a hand gently rest upon my back. As I looked up, I saw my good friend Jeanie. She didn't say anything, but her eyes spoke as if she could feel my pain through her touch. Later that day I received the following e-mail.

> Dearest Lynn,
>
> Please know that my thoughts and heart are with you. I cannot fathom how hard it is to come to worship without Bruce. I know God's hand is upon you. Even so, the pain and grief are real too. I will hold you up in prayer today and throughout the upcoming weeks. You are in a process that will take some time. Since the beginning of your news about Bruce's cancer, many of us had to consider how we would handle such a call from the Lord. I certainly don't feel ready or that my work is done here, and I am so incredibly attached to my family and friends. Isn't that part of the human equation?

But God is a jealous God, I am reminded, and we belong to Him first and foremost. He is our loving God and our haven, yet I tend to cling to the people in my life before I turn to Him. It is hard for me to imagine life here without my loved ones. My heart is with you. I have watched you and Bruce, as we all have, go forward with each step in faith. I have rarely seen anyone impact so many lives.

I was at the dentist office with my daughter, Jennifer, the other day. I was talking with a friend who came out and was sharing how the funeral touched her life. Before I knew it, another woman I don't know said, "I was there too. It changed my life forever." That is quite a statement! God will continue to bear good fruit from the work that you and Bruce have done toward His Kingdom! I didn't get a chance to ask who she was, but she knows the two of you. The big message is that she was touched so deeply that her life is forever changed . . . in a good way! Praise God! I hope that knowing this brings you some comfort. I pray that you can feel God's tender touch and His mighty hand all at the same time in the upcoming days. I know how much you love Bruce and how much he loved you. That is something that you will never lose. And that promise of our eternal reunion becomes more meaningful each day as I think of where we are all headed.

Hugs to you, Blake, and Nicole. Our prayers will continue without ceasing!

With God's love and with our friendship, Jeanie and family

This e-mail and others in the days to follow helped the bumpy road ahead become smoother as we encountered all the "firsts." I thank God for my wonderful friends and the treasures they are to me.

The Firsts

Until you lose your spouse you don't realize how truly blessed you are. Sound funny? I think not. As far as I could see, I was the luckiest and most blessed girl in the world. In many ways, according to societal views, Bruce and I had it all. Life without Bruce was hard, yet my life felt full and complete. The old saying, "You don't realize what you have until it's gone," bore new meaning. God knew what he was doing when he hooked us up in a Speech Communication class at SCSU many years ago. What one lacked the other had; and if not, then we relied heavily on the third strand in our marriage rope. He never failed us.

Despite the tragedy of cancer in Bruce's life, he won. In human eyes we see the tragedy, but when we allow ourselves to be vulnerable and comprehend God's way, we see the triumph.

The "firsts" were the hardest. My birthday was the "first." The kids relied on their dad to take them shopping. Not having him here made them sad. The same thing happened on Mother's Day.

There were other "firsts"—when I went grocery shopping and didn't need to buy the special foods for Bruce's unique diet; sitting in church on May 4th and realizing that it had already been one month since Bruce died; sitting alone at the kid's school musical where Blake had a lead role. *I sure missed Bruce then.*

The first time I bought fertilizer for our lawn. I stood in front of the multitude of fertilizer bags and realized I had no idea what to buy. I shot an arrow prayer up to God for some help, only to turn around and find Jim Stueve from church standing right there. What an immediate answer to prayer. There were so many other firsts: mowing the lawn alone and letting the Toro know who was going to win the battle. Going to Bruce's parent's cabin on Memorial Day (which held so many memories), asking Grandpa to teach Blake how to fillet the fish because Bruce always did that and would have taught Blake. The list goes on.

As tough as it was, God carried the kids and me. He intentionally made His presence known in our new journey. One of those ways came on my birthday. God surprised me in a way I would have never dreamed. My birthday came right after Bruce's funeral, and despite the efforts of others, I was incredibly blue. The kids and I had been to Kyle's for Easter. We stayed over night and then returned home on Easter Monday, which was my birthday. Before we went home, I drove to the cemetery. I felt bad because I hadn't had time to get flowers for the grave. I also needed to pick out a tombstone. Nothing was fair.

When we arrived home, we found a package at the front door. The package was from PJ in Florida. She was a friend of Bruce's while they studied abroad with other SCSU students in England. They were like family. I didn't know PJ, yet she wrote a beautiful note. She felt sad after he died. She had painted a picture of Bruce with his arms lifted high in praise. Golden highlights and unbelievable colors rained down upon him. He had what looked like angel wings boldly stretching out in majestic glory. The painting was an inspiration to me. It gave me great comfort knowing I now had a "before" and an "after" picture of Bruce. I praise God for the "after"!

When I first saw the painting, I was baffled as to why PJ had painted Bruce from the back side. Then it hit me—he is no longer looking back from where he is. Every time I look at the painting, which now hangs above my living room fireplace, I marvel at how God spoke so beautifully to me on my birthday through PJ and her paintbrush.

Another example of God's presence was on the day that would have been our 17th wedding anniversary. I woke up with a song playing repeatedly in my head. That song had haunted me ever since Bruce died—it was the song Bruce wanted played at his funeral. It wasn't until our anniversary that I awoke at Moms, and the song came to me. Quickly, I wrote the lyrics down on a piece of paper and tucked it into a safe place. There was no way I was going to let this one slip through my mind again. It reminded me of the first time I ever heard the song.

It had been on one of our drives to Parker Hughes, Bruce blurted out, "Lynn, you've got to listen to this song." It played on Christian radio. I looked over at Bruce and watched as he gently pounded his chest with a tightly closed fist. He tried to sing along, as tears streamed down his cheeks. When the song finished he said, "Lynn, do you realize what Jesus did for me, for Bruce MacKenzie? I never deserved it, but he died for *me*—above all! The price has been paid in full! Isn't that great, Lynn?"

"Yes, Bruce, it is."

"I want this song sung at my funeral someday; you know, some day when I'm in my 70s or 80s." Then, with a tear stained face, he smiled at me.

Later that day, I had lunch with two friends. I told them about the song and showed them the lyrics. My friend Jane's eyes got big. She just beamed!

"I know this song, Lynn! It's called *Above All*, and it's by Michael W. Smith from his Worship CD. I have it!" That afternoon, Jane brought the CD over to my mom's house. God is so amazing.

Who would have imagined the painting would arrive on my birthday? Or that on our 17th wedding anniversary I would wake up to the very song I so desperately wanted to remember? That, my friends, is God's grace.

The Dance Continues

One year after Bruce died, I received a note from a special friend. My encounter with Barb was brief, but it was clear that God orchestrated it. The note read:

Dear Lynn:

Last year while your husband was drawing nearer to his Lord,
You shared a beautiful story with your "sisters in Christ."
It was a memory of when you and Bruce danced.
This inspired me,
and it has lingered in my mind, heart, & soul—
then,
today,
and it will the rest of my days.
I simply wanted you to know how God has passed through
you to me.
With this I thank you for sharing.
My hope for you and your children is . . . that . . . —always,
I hope you Dance!

Keep the faith, Barb

Included with her note was a CD by Lee Ann Womack who sings *I Hope You Dance*. It is an inspiring song that spoke to me at a time when I needed to remember. It also encouraged me to keep living life, to keep dancing. Bruce would have wanted that. Even though he is gone and I am here, life is still out there for me to grab a hold of. For me, life is no longer about waiting for the storms to pass. It's about learning to dance in the rain.

The Reflection

Another May 10th arrived, and it had been three years since Bruce died. In the silence of our living room, I sat rocking in my recliner. I reflected back on time, contemplating all that had happened.

Reaching into my blue jean pocket to retrieve a tissue, my fingers fumbled onto something else I often carried around. It was that silly puzzle piece Pastor Craig Moore had given me. Flipping the bright yellow puzzle piece over and over between my fingers, I realized that not only was today Bruce's and my wedding anniversary, but also it would have been our 20th wedding anniversary. *Wow.* That event alone would have been another amazing puzzle piece I should have added to my puzzle; but, it wasn't. In fact, I no longer have the same puzzle. This piece represented the start to my new puzzle.

When Bruce took his last breath on earth, he was given the final piece to his puzzle. It was complete. Pieces were left behind. We have the memories.

My attention turned toward the family portrait above our upright piano. *What a nice picture,* I thought, but then I realized how much it had changed. There were only three members now. *Bruce will never again be in any of our family portraits.* That was crushing.

I focused back on the puzzle piece, and I realized he will always be a part of our puzzle. I felt sad but also a release. It was okay to move on.

I knew it was okay to go forward with my new puzzle—after all, new pieces were handed to me continually. I had faith that with God's help the pieces would fit together as He intended.

Just as God was faithful to Bruce, so He will be with me. It doesn't matter where I am in my journey—whether it's the beginning, somewhere in-between, or the end. When God gives me my last puzzle piece, I too will be able to confidentially say, "Hey, either way—I *win!*"

I said, *"God, I hurt"*
And God said, *"I know"*
I said, *"God I am so depressed"*
And God said, *"That's why I gave you sunshine"*
I said, *"God, life is so hard"*
And God said, *"That is why I gave you loved ones"*
I said, *"God, my loved one died"*
And God said, *"So did mine"*
I said, *"God, it is such a loss"*
And God said, *"I saw mine nailed to a cross"*
I said, *"God, but your loved one lives"*
And God said, *"So does yours"*
I said, *"God, where are they now?"*
And God said, *"Mine is on my right and yours is in the light"*

—author unknown

Bruce A. MacKenzie

Epilogue:
The Final Note

As I reflect back over the last several years, I never thought I would be in the place I am today. Nor did I think that I would get here this way.

The children and I are thriving. My son, Blake, has graduated from high school and is planning for college. Nicole is in high school, readily asks for the car keys, and is growing into a beautiful young lady. God has been prevalent in our lives. Over one year ago, I became the interim administrator for Prince of Peace Lutheran School, the school Bruce dedicated his final years to. I held the same position before at Trinity Lutheran School. That was the same year Bruce found out he had cancer. I look at both times served as "bookends." It was between the "bookends" that healing took place. Time *does* heal!

At some point, everyone asks the question, "Why?" about their lives. Why us? Why me? What purpose does my journey serve? What's the point?

In the days to come, I'm not sure where the Lord will lead me. I've learned to trust and follow Him, many times without knowing the answers to my questions. To live the abundant life requires action. That requires a total dependence and surrendering all.

Bruce always wanted me to write, and now I am. His response to his cancer diagnosis was, "Hey, either way, I win!" Through Bruce's words and the puzzle piece, God gave me a vision for a ministry called *I Win Ministries*. Its mission is to help hurting people and offer them hope. If this book and ministry, perhaps future books, and speaking engagements touch one lost soul, then all that brought me to this point will be worth it.

I told you earlier that the Lord led my good friend and cancer survivor, Carmen Britz, back into our lives. It wasn't just to minister to Bruce while he battled cancer. It was for a much greater purpose. I originally wrote the poem *The Tear Catcher* for Carmen. Ironically, it was for both of us. God doesn't promise we won't have tears, but He does promise to be there to catch them. Carmen since has helped edit this book and has become an intrinsic part of *I Win Ministries*. I am enthralled with how God works behind the scenes and orchestrates His ultimate purpose in our lives.

Daily, I continue with hope to seek the Lord's face and His will for my life. In the meantime, Bruce dances with the saints that have gone before us. One day, I too will join them in the dance.

Until that day comes, I continue my new life—beyond the bookends.

Lynn, Blake, & Nicole MacKenzie